Critical Literacies
in the
PRIMARY CLASSROOM

Critical Literacies
in the
PRIMARY CLASSROOM

Michele Knobel
and
Annah Healy
(editors)

Primary English Teaching Association

National Library of Australia Cataloguing-in-Publication data

Critical Literacies in the Primary Classroom
ISBN 1 87 5622 28 4

1. Literacy. 2. Critical thinking. 3. Language arts
(Primary). I. Michele Knobel. II. Healy, Anna, 1950– .
III. Primary English Teaching Association (Australia).

372.474

First published October 1998
Copyright © Primary English Teaching Association 1998
Laura Street Newtown NSW 2042 Australia

Edited by Robin Hedditch
Cover and text design by Pamela Horsnell, Juno Creative Services
Typeset in 10/13 Candida by DOCUPRO, Sydney
Printed by Star Printery
21 Coulson Street Erskineville NSW 2043

Acknowledgments

The editors would like to acknowledge the useful and important feedback provided by Viv Nicholl-Hatton, Susan Cornish, Rosamund Else-Mitchell, Stephen Scorse, and PETA's board and readers, as well as by Rebecca Campbell and Roanna Marstrand-Gottle, Bachelor of Education students at the Queensland University of Technology. In addition, Eileen Honan's input into this collection has been invaluable.

Although we have tried to enact the principles of critical literacy in this collection in terms of including a range of contributors and classroom contexts, unforeseen circumstances have meant that the spread of student groups represented has been curtailed. We hope readers will bring their own understandings of cultural and linguistic diversity to the chapters in this book.

Permissions

The editors and publishers gratefully acknowledge the following who have granted permission to reproduce previously published material:

Rondor Music, (Australia) Pty Ltd:
"I am Woman", words and music by Helen Reddy and Ray Burton
(c) Copyright Irving Music Inc and Buggerlugs Music Inc
Administered in Australia and New Zealand by Rondor Music.

EMI Blackwood Music Inc:
"My Boyfriend's Back", words and music by Robert Feldman, Gerald Gottehrer
(c) Copyright 1963 (renewed 1991)
All Rights Reserved. International Copyright Secured.

Warner/Chappell Music Australia Pty Ltd:
"You Don't Own Me", words and music by John Madara/Dave White
(c) Coyright Merjoda Music Inc/Unichappell Music Inc
For Australia & New Zealand:-
Warner/Chappell Australia Pty Ltd
3 Talvera Road North Ryde NSW 2113
International Copyright Secured. All Rights Reserved.
Unauthorised Reproduction Is Illegal.

Hodder Headline, Australia:
Loco-Zombies by Bill Condon and Robert Hood,
(c) Copyright 1996. pp. 46-47.

Fourth Estate Ltd:
Pythagoras' Trousers by Margaret Weirtheim.
Copyright (c) 1995 by Continents Music, Inc. Foreword copyright (c) 1996 by Margaret Weirtheim.

Allan Luke and Peter Freebody:
'The Social Practices of Reading' in *Constructing Critical Literacies*, edited by S. Muspratt, A. Luke and P. Freebody.
(c) Copyright 1997. p. 205.

Barbara Kamler:
'The Grammar Wars' appearing in *English in Australia*.
(c) Copyright 1995. pp. 9-10.

Myer Direct:
1998 Winter Values Catalogue, 1998.

Daniel Bowen:
Citation from http:///www.toxiccustard.com/australia/culture/html.

While every effort has been made to trace copyright holders, in some cases this has proven impossible. The editors and publisher apologise for such cases of unwilling copyright transgression and would like to hear from any copyright holders not acknowledged.

CONTENTS

Notes on Contributors — xi

CHAPTER 1
Critical literacies: An introduction — 1
Michele Knobel and Annah Healy

CHAPTER 2
Experts in Smurfland — 13
Jennifer O'Brien

CHAPTER 3
The Woody Kids — 27
Annah Healy

CHAPTER 4
A woman's place: A discussion of the place of linguistic analysis in the upper primary school — 41
Peter Wignell

CHAPTER 5
Theory and spice, and things not nice: Popular culture in the primary classroom — 53
Ray Misson

CHAPTER 6
'When you only have girls as friends, you got some serious problems': Interrogating masculinities in the literacy classroom — 63
Wayne Martino

CHAPTER 7
Words and life: Critical literacy and cultural action — 73
Chris Searle with Michele Knobel

CHAPTER 8
Critical literacy in teacher education — 89
Michele Knobel

CHAPTER 9
Literacy and critical reflection — 113
Colin Lankshear

GLOSSARY — 127
Michele Knobel and Eileen Honan

Notes on contributors

ANNAH HEALY
Annah Healy is a lecturer in the School of Language and Literacy Education, Queensland University of Technology. She has been working in the area of literacy and language education as a university educator, consultant, researcher and in the primary classroom for twenty five years. She believes that as texts and the constitution of literacies change, so must the approach to literacy education, to ensure the preparation of students for their futures.

MICHELE KNOBEL
Dr Michele Knobel is currently a lecturer in the School of Language and Literacy Education, Queensland University of Technology. She is deeply interested in primary students' everyday literacy practices in school and out-of-school and what this can tell us about constructing effective literacy learning content and contexts. She is the author of *Everyday Literacies: Students, Discourse, and Social Practice*. From 1999 onwards, Michele will be living somewhere in Mexico.

COLIN LANKSHEAR
Colin Lankshear is Professor of Education at the Queensland University of Technology. He has authored, co-authored, and co-edited numerous books on critical literacy themes, including *Literacy, Schooling and Revolution*, *Critical Literacy: Politics, Praxis and the Postmodern*, *The New Work Order*, and *Changing Literacies*. He will be migrating to Mexico in 1999.

WAYNE MARTINO
Dr Wayne Martino lectures in the Institute of Education at Murdoch University, Perth, Western Australia. He is currently working on a book entitled *Schooling Masculinities* with Maria Pallotta-Chiarolli which will be published late next year with Open University Press.

RAY MISSON
Dr Ray Misson is a Senior Lecturer in Language and Literacy Education and Associate Dean of the Faculty of Education in the University of Melbourne. He has written extensively on the implications of literary and cultural theory for the classroom, especially in relation to critical literacy and the teaching of popular culture.

JENNIFER O'BRIEN
When Jennifer O'Brien started teaching, popular culture had no official place at school. Unofficially, of course, it was everywhere, in classrooms as well as in the playground. When 'the popular' began to sneak in, and even to gain an official place, she spent a good deal of enjoyable and

productive time with young students exploring and challenging the delights of mass market texts. She has written about some of these experiences for educational policy documents, for journals, including *The Australian Journal of Language and Literacy*, and for several books about critical literacy and social justice issues due to be published in 1998 and 1999.

As a university researcher, her interests now include investigating how teachers make use of opportunities offered by official policy documents (such as the English *Statement* and *Profile*) to work and play with 'the popular'. Watching, reading and talking about popular culture continue to be personal as well as professional pleasures.

CHRIS SEARLE

Chris Searle has been a teacher for over 30 years. He has taught in east London, the Caribbean, Canada, Mozambique and Sheffield. His wide-ranging experience includes leading the Teacher Education program in Grenada and a five year period as headteacher of a Sheffield inner-city comprehensive school. He is currently a lecturer of English in Education in the postgraduate secondary program at Goldsmiths University of London. His latest book is titled *None But Our Words: Critical Literacy in Classroom and Community*, published with the Open University Press.

PETER WIGNELL

Peter Wignell is a lecturer in Applied Linguistics in the Faculty of Education at the Northern Territory University. He has, for a number of years, worked and published in the areas of literacy and literacy pedagogy. His published work includes *Critical Literacy: A Linguistic Perspective*, and the co-authored *Making Sense of Functional Grammar*.

CHAPTER 1

Critical literacies: An introduction

MICHELE KNOBEL AND ANNAH HEALY

Finding a place to begin a discussion about critical literacy is no easy task. Colin Lankshear (1997: 40–62) alerts teachers to some of the complications surrounding current pushes for critical literacy in classrooms. This includes what he calls the 'Magic Bullet syndrome', whereby the term 'critical literacy' is inserted into curriculum and policy documents in the seeming hope that this will be enough to overcome certain educational problems (eg inequitable schooling outcomes for certain cultural and social groups of students, such as Aborigines and Torres Strait Islanders, girls, immigrants etc). Lankshear identifies another complication, labelling it 'Everybody's Baby syndrome'. This problem is that almost everybody promotes critical literacy practices as important educational goals, but not everyone agrees on what critical literacy *is* and on what its outcomes should be.

Our aim in this book is not to provide a final definition of critical literacy or a single, neat set of critical literacy practices for primary classrooms. Rather, our goal is to present different ways of *doing* critical literacy in connection with everyday literacy practices. Although there are shared similarities or 'family resemblances' among different approaches to critical literacy, each comes with its own set of procedures and values that are not necessarily more 'right' or 'wrong' than the others. Resemblances and differences are discussed later in this chapter.

In what follows, we discuss *what* critical literacy is and *why* primary school teachers in Australia, New Zealand and elsewhere are being asked to include it in their classroom programs. Consequently, this chapter is more openly theoretical than other chapters. Indeed, some readers may prefer to start from chapter 2 and then return here when they feel more comfortable with key critical literacy concepts and practices used in other chapters. This introductory chapter also includes a suggested list of academic texts for readers interested in exploring critical literacy theories in more depth. In addition, for readers new to critical literacy or those who are re-acquainting themselves with it, a glossary of key terms and concepts used appears at the end of this volume.

What is critical literacy?

Critical literacy is something of a chameleon, changing from context to context, and from one educational purpose to another. It has a number of aliases, and is known in different parts of the world as: critical language awareness, critical social literacy, critically-aware literacy, critical literacy awareness, and the like. Nevertheless, there are at least four family resemblances shared among different approaches to critical literacy that provide a useful starting place for identifying the key characteristics of critical literacy practices.

Some family resemblances

First, advocates of critical literacy seem convinced that language education can make a difference in students' lives', and particularly in the lives of students who generally fall outside what is known as the 'mainstream' (Luke and Freebody 1997). Of course, history has shown repeatedly that 'being literate' in a functional or 'basic' sense is never enough on its own to bring about large-scale changes in people's everyday lives. Nevertheless, teachers who subscribe to critical literacy have a stake in social change—no matter how small—and aim to encourage their students to investigate, question and even challenge relationships between language and social practices that advantage particular social groups over others (Gilbert and Taylor 1991: 133).

Second, critical literacy approaches to language education assume that *meanings* of words and texts (and by 'texts' we mean 'stretches of language' which can be verbal, digital, printed, iconographic; anything that is 'coded' or belongs to a system of meaning) cannot be separated from the cultural and social practices in which—and by which—they are constructed. That is, language is used by all sorts of people to get all sorts of things done on a moment-by-moment basis, as well as in a more enduring sense, so that language—and literacy—is *fully* involved in social, historical, political and economic practices. Critical literacy practitioners accept that language—and the way that we use language to read, write, view, speak and listen—is never neutral or value-free.

Christine Walton (1993), for example, traces assumptions about language and schooling that have worked to deny Aboriginal people access to, and equality in, literacy education in Australia. She studied young Northern Territory Aboriginal children learning to write in an urban English-medium program by means of process writing and 'experience-based' models of teaching. She found these approaches assumed that all students came to school with the same 'literate cultural background'; that is, they had all read the same kinds of children's books in the same kinds of ways. This was certainly not the case for any of the Aboriginal students participating in the study, whose family life was deeply grounded in rich oral, kinesthetic and symbolic traditions. Cases like this remind us that language and literacy learning is not made up of neutral or impartial learning activ-

FIGURE 1.1: Re-viewing the world

ities and content that reward 'hard working' or 'smart' students (see Heath 1983). Even practices as seemingly benign as reading a picture book to young students is a culturally and politically complex act (Luke, Comber and O'Brien 1996: 34):

> through selections of textbooks, genres, children's literature, media, literate tastes and practices, dominant, mainstream cultures are assembled, presented and taught as culture [or as 'normal']. In this way, a selective tradition of culture is 'naturalised' as 'the way things are', 'that which we all believe', 'of universal appeal to all human beings' and so forth.

The chapters in this book take nothing for granted, and suggest ways of breaking down—or breaking out of—classroom language and texts as though they depict or resonate with 'the way things are' for everybody.

Third, critical literacy is about analysing and evaluating *something*. Ira Shor (1992: 32), for example, emphasises the key roles of analysis and critique in critical literacy. For him, critical literacy is:

> analytic habits of thinking, reading, writing, speaking, or discussing which go beneath surface impressions, traditional myths, mere opinions, and routine clichés; *understanding the social contexts and consequences* of any subject matter; discovering the deep meaning of any event, text, technique, process, object, statement, image, or situation; applying that meaning to your own context [our emphasis].

Analysis and evaluation of texts goes beyond simply recognising that they are not neutral and value-free to look at how some texts fit more easily with the experiences of particular groups of readers and writers and their views of the world. Indeed, *all* texts—whether conventional print, video, digital or whatever—promote certain versions or representations of a particular 'reality'. Hilary Janks (1993: iii) signals this when she declares, 'what makes critical language awareness [or critical literacy] "critical" is its concern with the politics of meaning: the ways in which dominant meanings are maintained, challenged and changed'. For example, Janks challenges black and white South African school students to think about how texts as everyday as maps are representations of a particular reality (not to mention history) by providing them with maps of the world that locate southern hemisphere countries at the 'top' of the map, instead of in their usual, often assumed position at the 'bottom' of the map.

Ensuing discussion often leads to talk about who gets to name—or change the name of—things and places, how this comes to be, and whose 'reality' or experiences this usually represents (Uluru/Ayers Rock is a case in point). From this angle, critical analysis—or interrogation—of texts is concerned with analysing the relationship between language (and literacy) practices and social practices, and the ways in which this relationship is always constituted and shaped over time by social groups who have greater access to power than other groups. In short, critical literacy involves analysing relationships between language, social groups, social practices and power.

Fourth, some notion of what it means to be socially aware and active citizens permeates most of the writing on critical literacy (Lankshear and Knobel 1997). For example, Chris Searle (1993), one of our contributing authors, focuses on developing what he calls 'imaginative empathy' in his students. He uses a range of texts to encourage them to imagine themselves into the lives of others and to write poetry and prose from these different life views. Outcomes include books of professionally published poetry that work to challenge and perhaps shift the ingrained racial and class tensions that characterise their school and civic community. Other outcomes include groups of students and school community members organising functions to raise money to donate to families in trouble in Somalia or Ethiopia, rallying the larger community into cleaning up areas surrounding their inner-city school, or publicly protesting council and government policy changes that will disadvantage members of this community. Practised in this way, critical literacy is about *transforming* taken-for-granted social and language practices or assumptions for the good of as many people as possible (Freire 1972).

A word of caution

Taking a critical literacy stance in classroom practices is not a neutral act, but comes loaded with issues that need to be carefully considered and monitored by teachers. As Pam Gilbert notes (1993: 325), critical literacy 'means engaging with issues that are often controversial, certainly contemporary, and perhaps quite volatile'. For example, decisions need to be made as to how far to push—or enable students to push—a critique of texts, practices and institutions (see Ray Misson's chapter). Schools play a strong normative role in society and any actions that pose a serious threat to this role, to the institution itself, or even to other social institutions, invoke angry responses and reprisals that may have long-term effects on the livelihoods of all involved (see Chris Searle's chapter). Teachers also need to reflect continuously on how they themselves are constructing what 'counts' as critical literacy in their classroom and what stance

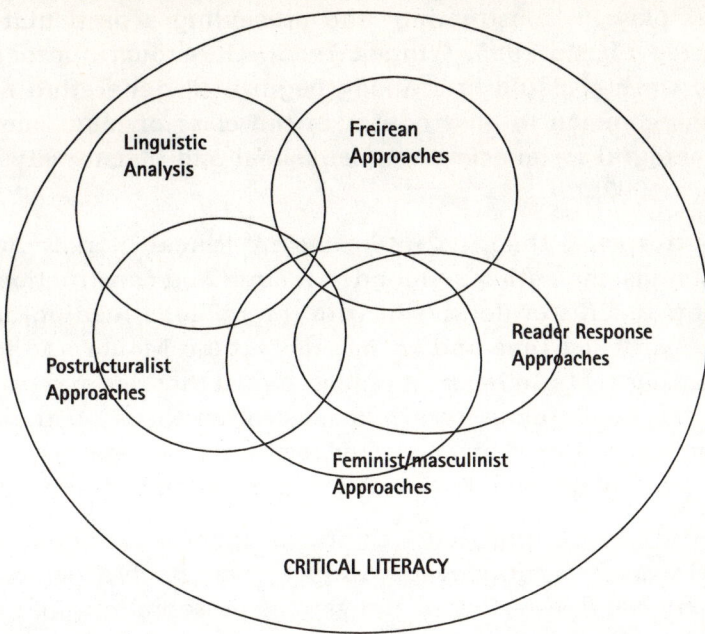

FIGURE 1.2: Different theoretical approaches to critical literacy

they are wittingly or unwittingly expecting students to take on social issues. Care must be taken that the teacher is not really engaging in a form of political manipulation, but instead in activities of analysis and critique that are open to discussion and different, or multiple, points of view.

Likewise, cultural and social sensitivity must accompany critical literacy practices and expectations in any classroom. For example, a teacher who has students from cultural or religious backgrounds who hold strong beliefs about the role of women in the family would need to think very carefully about her or his students when planning a unit designed to challenge gender roles in narratives. To assume that the 'Western' feminist version of gender is the 'right' or 'best' way to approach who does what in all families is to ignore the complexity of different 'constructions' of families in different cultures, and may result in creating tensions in students' lives that interfere with family and school relations in ultimately disadvantaging ways. The chapters in this book will draw your attention to ethical problems and other issues attached to critical literacy, but cannot provide 'quick-fix' solutions.

Points of difference

Having dealt so far with some of the shared components of critical literacy approaches to classroom practice, it is useful at this point to differentiate among them. It will become apparent as you read through the chapters in this book that different approaches to critical literacy foreground different sets of issues, and theoretical positions or understandings. For example, approaches that employ functional grammar in analysing written texts emphasise the roles grammatical structures and linguistic choices play in 'constructing' and presenting a particular version of the world (eg Martin 1993, Wignell 1996). Classroom approaches that build on the work of Paulo Freire may begin with generating and exploring a problem common to all students in the class or may focus on some sort of meaningful social action (eg Lankshear and McLaren 1993, Searle 1998, Wallace 1992b).

Reader-response theorists interested in critical literacy question, among other things, the author's 'intended reader' and construction of social roles, and how this fits or doesn't fit with the reader's reading or interpretation at that particular time and in that context (eg Mellor and Patterson 1996). Approaches that use feminist or masculinist theories and principles to challenge the assumptions of a text most often focus on the ways in which genders are portrayed and allocated to characters or participants in a reported event (eg Gilbert and Taylor 1991, Martino and Mellor 1994).

Post-structuralist approaches to critical literacy in the classroom are concerned usually with analysing the ways in which a person's or a character's 'subjectivities'—that is, the various presentations and representations of one's 'self' or 'subjecthood'—are represented in texts in ways that are constraining, liberating, 'silencing', or empowering, and so on (eg Davies 1993, Morgan et al 1996). 'Discourse' approaches to critical literacy generally argue that patterns of speaking, acting, writing, reading, being, dressing, thinking and the like 'belong' to, or characterise, different groups of people, and that these patterns are always historical and social, and work to privilege some groups over others (eg Fairclough 1992, Gee 1996, Lankshear 1997). Of course, this listing is not exhaustive and, as you will see in the following chapters, these and other approaches often overlap or merge in the work of different researchers and writers.

Differences among the various approaches to critical literacy can be attributed in large part to the theories that inform them. Differences are also generated by the assumptions about literacy that underpin each approach, and by the ways in which these assumptions are played out in terms of what teachers and students *do* with texts and *how* they go about it. Lankshear provides a useful framework for examining some of these differences.

Three takes on critical literacy approaches

Lankshear (1997: 44) proposes three takes on critical literacy, basing his analysis on what is critiqued (ie the 'object' of critique) in different approaches. Accordingly, a critical literacy might involve any or all of:

- 'having a critical perspective on [language and] *literacy* or *literacies per se*, where literacy itself is the object of critique;
- having a critical perspective on particular *texts,* where the critique of texts and their worldviews is the object;
- having a critical perspective on—i.e., being able to analyse and critique—wider *social practices* . . . etc. which are mediated by,

made possible, and partially sustained through reading, writing, viewing, transmitting, etc., texts. Here, social practices, their histories, their normative work, and their associated literacy practices and artifacts, etc., are the target of analysis and critique'.

A critical perspective on language and literacy

A critical perspective on language involves knowing language for what it is; that is, as a social practice, and for what it can get done in the world: 'It is through language that we come to an understanding of our world, and it is through language that our world is constructed. We therefore need to consider critically what and how we learn about our world (including ourselves) through reading, writing and talking' (O'Brien 1994: 36). This applies equally to literacies. Lankshear discusses this 'knowing' in terms of developing a *meta-level understanding* of the ways in which literacies are part and parcel of sets of language (ie 'discourses', with a lower case *d*) and social practices (what he and others call 'Discourses', with a capital *D*; see Gee 1996). In simple terms, having a meta-level understanding of language is to *know* that people interact using a convention- or rule-governed system of communication (ie language), and to *understand* that language (and literacy) is more than a fixed system of sounds and symbols; instead, it is an indissoluble part of everyday social practices. Meta-level understanding of language is what Gunther Kress describes as *knowing* language and *knowing about* language (1985: 31).

A critical/evaluative perspective on texts

Texts are more than just collections of words and sentences; they are also *ideological*. For our purposes in this book, we define *ideology* as a social theory or worldview which involves generalisations (beliefs, claims) about the ways in which the world 'works' (see Gee 1996: 21). Ideologies are tied closely to distributions of power and access to goods and services in any society. Ideology is not necessarily a conscious or deliberate act on the author's part, nor is it necessarily tied to indoctrination or to potentially harmful acts. Nevertheless, it is important to be able to identify ideologies operating in texts, and to be aware of the ways in which ideologies inform and shape authors' concepts and word choices—and the meanings these choices embody, construct and promote—in order to be as aware as possible of what we are 'buying into' when we read a text and agree with or accept what the author is saying (and how it is being said) without question.

Classroom approaches to critical literacy that promote a critical perspective on particular texts usually emphasise analysing and evaluating authors' world views and/or their constructions of 'reality'. This dimension of critical literacy is interested in generating new texts in response to a particular version of the world constructed or assumed in a given text (eg a world where darker skinned people are less 'developed' or 'civilised' than lighter skinned people). These responses generally aim at rewriting texts in ways that promote alternative views of the world that are more culturally inclusive and just.

Having a critical perspective on texts is about much more than having the technical skills to analyse texts (although, as we indicated above, critical thinking skills and processes like analysing, synthesising, extrapolating, evaluating etc are important). Critical literacy and critical thinking are not necessarily synonymous activities. As mentioned earlier, critical literacy is grounded in sociocultural theories, and a shorthand definition for it is the analysis and critique of relationships among language, power, social groups and social practices. Key concepts in any definition of critical literacy are 'power' and 'social critique'. Readers may also be familiar with the terms 'critical pedagogy' and 'critical reading'. To cut a complex story short, 'critical pedagogy' is generally used to refer to the strategies and processes teachers use to teach or enact critical literacy in their classrooms (see the glossary at the end of this book). If we think about critical literacy as a 'coverall' practice, then critical reading is a specific process within it (just as there is also 'critical writing' etc; see the glossary).

On the other hand, critical thinking is grounded in psychological theories, or theories of how the mind works (eg those found in cognitive science studies). In short, critical thinking is usually defined as the 'ability to think about one's thinking' in order to improve it (Paul 1995). This includes remembering facts, using effective habits of thinking that require little mental effort, using processes of inquiry (to reach conclusions), generating new ideas and thinking creatively (OISE 1997). More specifically, critical thinking is seen as part and parcel of *processing information*, which includes 'knowledge application, analysis, synthesis, reasoning, problem solving, decision making, and evaluation' (Crowley 1996). In education, critical thinking is often talked about and practised in constructivist approaches to teaching and learning.

So, you need, among other things, critical thinking to do critical literacy, but you can do critical thinking without doing critical literacy (ie without critiquing social and power relationships etc). Popular movie and book reviews are a case in point. These texts are evaluations of the quality of another text, requiring analysis, and often synthesis. However, these reviews rarely comment on, say, the power of Hollywood dollars and the movie industry in general and the effects of this power on movie-goers etc, or on the cultural assumptions screenwriters and directors choose to make or depict and the ideologies they promote.

It is imperative that teachers are aware of the distinction between critical thinking and critical literacy, particularly in the light of recent pushes in the business sector, for example, that promote the need for employees who are able to solve problems, be troubleshooters and think divergently for the 'good' of the business, but not necessarily for the 'good' of the workers (ie owners and managers certainly do not want workers who are able to critique, and act on their critique, of the company in relation to its workers, national economies, globalisation, and so on. See Gee,

Lankshear and Hull 1996). Collapsing the distinction between critical literacy and critical thinking does students a grave disservice.

A critical perspective on social practices

Unfortunately, teaching approaches grounded in critical literacy perspectives sometimes assume that changing the ways in which language and texts are used will almost automatically change social practices. Having a critical perspective on *social practices*—Lankshear's third take on approaches to critical literacy—involves teachers and students in developing strategies for addressing the *social contexts* of literacy practices and the networks of power that are created and sustained by these literacy practices. For example, 11-year-old students in one of Chris Searle's classes critiqued luxury hotel development in the docklands area of their working class district in London (see Searle 1998: 65; also Chapter 7 in this book). The students examined the tariffs of the hotel and wrote poems in response to the social inequities they encountered in their everyday lives and that were symbolised by the hotel. These poems, and others critiquing the general gentrification of the area (which also included the closing of a local public hospital), were formally published in a collection called *Classrooms of Resistance*, and drew widespread attention to the groups of developers who were moving in and taking over this community at the expense of adequate, low-cost housing, accessible health care, and the like.

Hopefully the discussion so far has provided some basic frameworks or criteria for identifying and understanding different approaches to critical literacy. The next section begins to address a question we often hear from teachers and student teachers: 'Why do critical literacy?'

Why do critical literacy?

Increasingly, it seems, teachers are expected to include critical literacy approaches in their classroom literacy work. Indeed, expectations are built into subject English policies and syllabi, but rationales for these expectations are often glossed over. In many cases, it is possible to source these expectations in national economic development agendas that make causal links between 'critically-aware literacy' and economic competitiveness (see, for example, *Australian Literacies* 1997: 22). Working with a much wider rationale, however, we want to emphasise the potential social benefits of doing critical literacy in primary school classrooms. We are deeply interested in, and committed to, addressing disadvantage and injustice—particularly as experienced by our students—in as many ethical ways as possible. This is particularly important for us at present in the face of the increased push for skills-based approaches to literacy learning at the expense of other, effective approaches. Skills-based approaches work to remove literacy learning from real world contexts by constructing language and literacy as a fixed, neutral system of language rules, symbols and conventions, rather than locating it within a broader matrix of power, history, schooling, culture, class, and so on. To provide students with a knowledge only of language, and not a meta-level understanding of how language works, is to only give them part of the picture. Kress (1985) refers to the latter process as learning about the world and its ways *through* (meta-level understandings of) language.

Understanding classroom approaches to critical literacy, especially for teachers new to the practice, is not exactly helped by many policy syllabus documents where the term 'critical' is used to mean different things but without clear differentiation between meanings. For example, *Australian Literacies* uses *critical* to mean 'something important', 'higher order thinking strategies', and 'an issue', as well as in the sense that permeates this book. A look at statements that deal with 'analysing texts critically' in the national English profile (Australian Education Council 1994) suggests that the writers are more interested in technical text analysis and book reviews than in critiquing, say, the 'ideal readers' or ideologies of texts. This has significant implications for teachers when they follow to the letter critical literacy directives promoted in policy and syllabus documents.

We believe teachers should be very clear about *why* they are doing critical literacy in their classrooms, and about the outcomes they hope to achieve. This can be helped by critiquing the use of the term 'critical literacy' in texts that make claims on its behalf (including this book). This kind of critique can be assisted by asking and answering questions such as the following:

- How is literacy being defined in this text? (eg as a decontextualised skill? As a social practice?)

- How is the term 'critical' being used in this text? (eg if I take the word 'critical' out of the text, what differences does it make? What synonyms could meaningfully replace the way 'critical' is used in this paragraph, and what does this tell me?)

- What other concepts are discussed in relation to, or as part of, critical literacy in this text? (eg is critical literacy talked about only within the context of texts, or are social contexts and concepts included?)

- In this text, what processes are associated with the practice of critical literacy? (Is the enactment of critical literacy discussed as an individual or as a group/community process? Is it grounded in sociocultural theory?)

All too easily, critical literacy can become a bandwagon to hitch a ride on, without necessarily going anywhere productive, or worse, can be put to use carting educational practices that are incompatible with the values and goals of effective critical literacy education. We hope that this collection of approaches to critical literacy goes at least some way towards encouraging informed and effective approaches to critical literacy in primary school classrooms.

How is critical literacy done?

The following eight chapters present practical ideas, strategies, techniques and tools for implementing critical literacy approaches to literacy in primary school classrooms. In chapter 2, Jennifer O'Brien uses a popular mass-market text with her Reception to Year 2 students to question the construction of female gender roles in a particular series of books. Annah Healy, in chapter 3, presents snapshots of a Year 5 classroom where the lines between formal schooling and the community are blurred in ways that challenge traditional 'schoolish' approaches to literacy. A range of effective strategies for working with popular culture in a critical literacy classroom are provided by Ray Misson in chapter 5, and Wayne Martino models a useful process for challenging mainstream and homophobic conceptions of masculinity in chapter 6. In chapter 7 Chris Searle, with Michele Knobel, evocatively describes how to bring together critical literacy, writing, and social action in the classroom. In chapter 8 Michele Knobel presents a number of practical activities she uses in teaching Bachelor of Education students about critical literacy and how to teach it. In the final chapter, Colin Lankshear reminds teachers to reflect on their *own* literacy practices and assumptions in relation to critical literacy and classroom practice.

To sum up, the strategies and activities presented in these chapters are not meant to be bags of tricks or prescriptions for practice, but are intended as *guides* to what works for certain teachers in contexts that may resonate with your own circumstances. Implementing these suggestions will require reflection, analysis and input from literacy and social theories, otherwise 'doing' critical literacy will simply become just another way of 'doing school'.

Read in conjunction with the ideas presented in this introduction, each chapter demonstrates that critical literacy is not a bag of tricks, but an active demonstration of the relationship between theory and practice, and emphasises the importance of being a reflective practitioner.

References

Australian Education Council (1994) *English: A Curriculum Profile For Australian Schools.* Carlton: Curriculum Corporation.

Crowley, J (1996) Critical Thinking in the Laboratory: Key Word List. Cited 8 July, 1998. http://158.93.30.93/MedTech/LL/CT/KEYWORDS.HTM

Davies, B (1993) *Shards of Glass: Children Reading and Writing Beyond Gendered Identities.* Sydney: Allen and Unwin.

Freire, P (1972) *Pedagogy of the Oppressed.* Harmondsworth: Penguin Education.

Gee, J (1996) *Social Linguistics and Literacies: Ideology in Discourses.* London: Falmer Press.

Gee, J, Lankshear, C and Hull, G (1996) *The New Work Order*. Sydney: Allen and Unwin.

Gilbert, P (1993) (Sub)versions: Using sexist language practices to explore critical literacy. *Australian Journal of Language and Literacy*. Vol 16, No 4, pp 323–332.

Gilbert, P and Taylor, S (1991) *Fashioning The Feminine*. Sydney: Allen and Unwin.

Janks, H (1993) *Language and Position*. Sydney: Hodder and Stoughton.

Kress, G (1985) *Linguistic Processes in Sociocultural Practice*. Geelong: Deakin University Press.

Lankshear, C (1997) *Changing Literacies*. London: Open University Press.

Lankshear, C and Knobel, M (1997) 'Critical literacy and active citizenship', in A Muspratt, A Luke and P Freebody (1997) (eds) *Constructing Critical Literacies*. Cresskill: Hampton Press, pp 95–124.

Lankshear, C and McLaren, P (1993) (eds) *Critical Literacy: Politics, Praxis and the Postmodern*. Albany: State University of New York Press.

LoBianco, J (1997) *Australian Literacies*. Belconnen, ACT: Language Australia.

Luke, A and Freebody, P (1997) 'Critical literacy and the question of normativity', in A Muspratt, A Luke, and P Freebody (eds) *Constructing Critical Literacies*. Cresskill: Hampton Press, pp 1–18.

Luke, A Comber, B and O'Brien, J (1996) 'Critical literacies and cultural studies', in G Bull and M Anstey (eds) *The Literacy Lexicon*. pp 31–46.

Luke, C and Gore, J (1993) (eds) *Feminisms and Critical Pedagogy*. New York: Routledge.

Martin, J (1985) *Factual Writing: Exploring and Challenging Social Reality*. Geelong: University Press.

Martino, W and Mellor, B (1994) *Gendered Fictions*. Cottesloe: Chalkface Press.

Mellor, B and Patterson, A (1966) *Investigating Texts*. Cottesloe: Chalkface Press.

Morgan, W et al (1996) *Critical Literacy: Readings and Resources*. Australian Association for the Teaching of English.

O'Brien, J (1994) 'Critical literacy in an early childhood classroom: A progress report', *Australian Journal of Language and Literacy*. Vol 17, No. 1, pp 36–44.

OISE (Ontario Institute for Studies in Education) (1997) Critical Thinking. Cited July 8, 1998. http://www3.sympatico.ca/lgrightmire/CRITICAL.HTM

Paul, R (1995) 'Three Definitions of Critical Thinking'. Cited 7 July, 1998. http://www.sonoma.edu/cthink/definect.html

Wignell, P (1996) *Critical Literacy: A Linguistic Perspective*. Canberra: National Languages and Literacy Institute of Australia.

Collections

The Australian Journal of Language and Literacy (1993). Vol 16, No 4. Journal of the Australian Literacy Educators' Association.

Changing Education (1996). Vol 3, No 1. Deakin Centre for Educational Change Journal for Teachers and Administrators.

Interpretations (1990). Vol 30, No 1. Journal of the English Teachers' Association of Western Australia.

Idiom (1993). Vol 29, No 2. Journal of the Victorian Association of Teachers of English.

Open Letter (1995). Vol 6, No 4. The Australian Journal for Adult Literacy research and Practice.

CHAPTER 2

Experts in Smurfland

JENNIFER O'BRIEN

In this chapter, Jennifer O'Brien demonstrates the ways in which she develops critical reading skills in a Reception to Year 2 classroom. In doing so, she discusses 'textual authority', and how this authority is often entwined with the teacher's authority as a social role and as an expert reader. O'Brien describes how this relationship is disrupted in a reading session when she encourages students to take up positions of 'text experts' by foregrounding their cultural knowledge about mass-market texts, and about Smurf texts in particular. A feminist perspective on texts is developed through a specific line of questioning in ways that make space for students to demonstrate their knowledge of the text and its content, as well as for critically analysing the text and the world views it promotes.

> . . . it seems to me that the most critical requirement for a curriculum that . . . allows for the distinctiveness of the individual and of diverse cultural resources, is a teacher who conveys a respect for children and their communities, a respect that is actualised by listening and actively working to make curricular space for all students (Dyson 1992: 459).

> . . . reading in contemporary culture . . . requires flexible practices which enable critical engagement with new and innovative texts on a daily basis (Luke 1995: 181).

In this chapter I show how I interrupted common teacher–student roles of expert and novice to set up my young students in critical engagement with the mass-market text, *A Lady in Smurfland* (Peyo, n.d.). I didn't completely bail out of a 'expert' role, however. Instead, I set up a situation where students and I interpreted *A Lady in Smurfland* to each other. I had only the sketchiest knowledge of the 'Smurf world' myself. I therefore incorporated students' expertise as text users and participants (Freebody and Luke 1990) in Smurf products into the reading-aloud session, along with feminist theories and my understandings about texts aimed at young consumers. Although I use *A Lady in Smurfland* in this chapter to model the critical literacy work I do with young students, this model is designed to work equally well with other mass-market texts popular with children, such as those produced by the Disney corporation (eg *Pocahontas*, *Hercules*, *The Little Mermaid*), and the like.

As I read *A Lady in Smurfland* aloud, classroom discussion turned on the cultural meanings this book had in the lives of these children. Setting myself up as the novice in the matter of these texts of commercial culture (Dyson 1995) brought into play considerations of *intertextuality*. In other words, this move allowed classroom talk to focus on the ways in which *A Lady in Smurfland* is intimately linked not only to other texts but to other cultural products (in this particular case, a series of television shows) and to the lives of its readers. In turn, I used the social world created in *A Lady in Smurfland* to make commonsense understandings about love and marriage and topics for classroom talk.

The setting

Picture the scene . . . I'm sitting with my class of Reception to Year 2 students. We've just come back inside after a vigorous session on the climbing equipment. It's my usual practice to include a range of different texts in the classroom and to incorporate into reading aloud sessions various ways of using them. 'Who's brought something for me to read?' I ask.

Troy brings out *A Lady in Smurfland* and I hold it up. It's small and slim, with a stapled cardboard cover and brightly coloured illustrations. I note its low price, then mentally scan the cultural knowledge I bring to this book. There's not a great deal. I've seen other titles in the same series at the supermarket check-out counter, although I've never read one. A petrol company sponsors a vigorous television promotion of the books and spin-off figurines, so I'm aware that these commodities have a place in a commercial world rather than in the literary world. My own children are past the age for reading these particular mass-market titles so I haven't had to weigh up the potential enjoyment my children might gain from reading these books against my prejudice in favour of the sorts of books usually referred to as 'children's literature': texts written by well-regarded authors and illustrators, relatively expensive, sold in bookshops, and valued for their literary qualities rather than their commercial connections.

The cover shows what I take to be a female and a male Smurf. She's very blonde, with large lips; he's surrounded by hearts. Drawing on a feminist perspective, I assess the possibilities. I surmise that the narrative goes something like this: Smurfland is mainly the province of males; a stereotypical pretty female character comes on the scene; a male Smurf falls in love with her, provoking conflict among the males; marriage is the likely outcome.

The sounds of approval from students make it pretty clear that Smurf books are a familiar and pleasurable part of the children's everyday cultural world. My guesses are that parents, relatives and caregivers buy them as gifts when they're shopping; that some of the older children read them independently; that their parents or caregivers, and perhaps even older brothers or sisters, read them aloud at home; that they swap titles among themselves. Students might also collect the plastic figurines, watch the television series, drink from Smurf cups, eat from Smurf bowls, and sleep in the Smurf sheet-set. In short, my students are likely to be expert in a range of reading practices related to this book or similar titles.

Previously I might have rejected *A Lady in Smurfland*, telling Troy that books like this don't have a place in serious discussions in classrooms. Or I might have read it aloud, making no comment but silently finding fault with its sexist plot and mass-produced emotion and artwork. But on this occasion I read the book aloud, and invite students to discuss social and cultural meanings the text might have; that is, I invite students to join me in critically analysing the text. In this way, the reading session becomes an opportunity for the children to participate in the delight and pleasure afforded by *A Lady in Smurfland* while I help them to analyse and challenge what texts such as these, suggest about being female and male in contemporary life.

Why bother taking a Smurf book seriously? It is, after all, one of a group of mass-market texts produced for the consumption of young children. What am I going to do with this book, in this situation? My decisions are informed by critical perspectives on texts and readers, students and reading lessons.

Texts and readers

Like all texts, a mass-market title such as *A Lady in Smurfland* establishes relationships with its readers, often referred to as the way a text *positions* its readers. Relationships between texts and readers are the products of complex interactions influenced by many factors. These include the 'authority' carried by the text and the social and cultural knowledge and experiences of the reader.

Texts use various devices to suggest that 'this is the way things are' and to claim authority. Textual authority may be achieved by calling on time-honoured traditions of story patterning, by the way language is used, by the way words and graphics are put together, and by the content selected. However, textual authority is also maintained by readers who bring social and cultural resources to each text. These resources include troubled, pleasurable, or relatively neutral experiences with similar kinds of books, with reading in general, or with books in general. But readers' resources include knowledge about more than just the process of reading. For example, a reader who knows something about a book's topic or about links between book publishers, toy manufacturers and film distributors is in a different position from one who knows nothing. A reader who understands that 'people like me don't read books like this' brings yet another set of cultural resources to a reading. Readers therefore take up diverse positions towards, and readings of, the same books. And at different times in history, or in different social situations, texts can carry different meanings.

Take Smurf books, for example. For some children, interconnections between these books and a multiplicity of related products targeted at young consumers are deeply influential. Accordingly, the presence of Smurf books and artefacts in playground networks might create relatively strong links between children and between the 'cultural knowledge' that they share. Other children, however, will not have been captivated by 'the whole Smurf thing'. Similarly, it might be expected that a teacher has quite different sets of relationships with Smurf books, as might older children or children whose families discourage them from reading about Smurfs. So there's a complex interplay between the contexts in which texts are produced by writers and the ways in which they are received by readers.

In classrooms, another factor contributing to the authority of texts and readings comes into play: the teacher–student relationship around texts in general. Teachers often decide what aspects of texts will be discussed, and, despite appearing to ask young readers about their interpretations of classroom texts, usually give preference to their own views (Baker and Freebody 1989). In my reading lessons, therefore, I consciously aim at recasting this version of teacher-student relations so that we can negotiate, share and exchange roles as text authorities, cultural experts, inquirers, novices and co-makers of meaning.

Reading lessons, like other elements of the literacy curriculum, are places where students and teachers can work together at the serious business of grappling with texts of all kinds, including those of popular culture. They afford space where students build and deploy an adaptable set of practices towards reading lessons, towards school and out-of-school texts, and towards each other. Reading lessons are places from where children carry their repertoire of understandings about how texts work 'linguistically and politically' into the social world (Luke 1995: 184).

In reading lessons, and particularly in reading-aloud sessions, young children learn to join in conventionalised classroom talk about poetry, jokes, books, films and television shows. In these contexts they shape and re-shape the cultural resources they bring to schooling (Dyson 1993, 1995). However, children have different access to, and proficiencies with, classroom talk. Despite commonly held beliefs that literacy is a politically neutral accomplishment attainable pretty well universally by students of similar intellectual ability and motivation, children enter classrooms unevenly prepared for the teacher's cultural assumptions that inform his or her literacy teaching (Carrington and Luke 1997). For example, the intertextual resources (ie experiences with, and knowledge of, previous texts) and ways of reading that children bring to classrooms are valued and acknowledged differentially by classroom curricula and assessment practices.

Accordingly, in this chapter, I take a reading-aloud session built around Smurf books and television programs and show how the cultural resources of children's out-of-school lives both expand the literacy curriculum and become one of its distinctive features (Dyson 1995).

Possibilities for action

Students' familiarity with Smurf books and their evident pleasure in them are a wonderful but fragile starting point. In any discussion of texts with my students I want to create a space where critical engagement can take place without spoiling the fun in the text; I want to intervene but also to tread lightly. Let me suggest a few possibilities that match these aims.

I could focus on aspects of social and economic contexts in which Smurf books are read, swapped, purchased and so on, setting up an investigation into the marketing and consumption of popular mass-market titles. To do this, I might read the book aloud first, then use activities and questions such as:

1 Make a list of all the Smurf titles you can find and where you found them (eg at home, in a library, in a supermarket).

2 How long do you think Smurf books have been popular? What makes you think this? When did you first see a Smurf book?

3 How many class members own Smurf books? How many titles does each person have? Where did they get them? When? Why?

4 What do people do with Smurf books? Who with? Why?

5 Are there people who don't read Smurf books? Why don't they? (Ask adults as well as children.)

6 Where can you buy Smurf books? Why are they sold in these places?

7 Are Smurf books connected with other products, like toys or clothes? Make a list. See if you can find out who produces the toys and who produces the books. Are they connected in any way? Why?

8 Are Smurf books connected with other kinds of entertainment, like television shows? In what ways? Who were these shows made for, do you think? How do you know? Who watches these shows? When? Who with?

Alternatively, the texts themselves could be the focus. In this case, I might have students investigate how the series works to create particular versions of the social world by building a picture of the 'Smurf world' with questions such as:

1 Do the Smurf books all have the same characters?

2   What are the names of the characters?

3   What do you get to know about the characters by reading the books? (eg how they live, what they eat, what they wear).

4   Are Smurfs meant to be people or imaginary creatures?

5   In what ways do the Smurfs behave like people you know? In what ways not?

These two different sets of questions would generate a lot of rich information about Smurfs, their world, and social practices in students' own lives that are associated with them. These questions, or others like them, would be effective launch pads for units of work that develop and refine students' analyses and understandings even more. But that's another story.

A Lady in Smurfland

On this occasion, I aim at producing a multi-layered conversation about the book while I read it aloud. My feminist perspective and knowledge of mass-market books targeting young consumers suggest that the story line might turn on a stereotypical version of falling in love. With this assumption in mind, I intend to produce readings of the illustrations, the characters and the story line which interrupt assumptions that female and male characters should behave in particular ways on the basis of their gender—at least in the context of this book and others like it. At the same time, I want to create a space where the classroom talk is guided by students' experiences as users and consumers of Smurf texts and participants in the social world constructed in these books. I plan to position students as experts with Smurf texts and myself as novice in the Smurf department, but one with authority to ask questions and to guide the experts' discussion.

My work is premised on the idea that in reading lessons I contribute very particular understandings about texts, and therefore, my position should be made explicit to students. In every reading lesson I try to make it clear that I have certain 'perspectives' or theories that guide my understandings, and explain to my students where these perspectives came from. At the same time, I keep clearly in focus the idea that text meanings don't float free of a context, but are related to the specific text, who is reading it, and so on.

In the following discussion—based on a transcript produced from an audiotape of the lesson—I reveal some of the twists and turn of the talk, identify some of the leads followed and some of those ignored, and suggest other ways this multi-layered discussion could have gone.

Before I start reading *A Lady in Smurfland* aloud, I ask children to spend a few minutes in groups making predictions on the basis of the title, the front cover and their knowledge of what happens in other books they've read. I ask them to say what they think the female on the front cover will do in the story, what they expect the writer will tell them about this character and what they won't be told. My decision to ask 'What do you think *could* be in the book, but that won't be included?' is informed by the notion that what is *not* revealed throws light on the selective process used by writers when they're creating a social world in texts.

When students return to the whole-class group, I ask for a review of the small-group conversations. I soon find that the children bring to the lesson cultural knowledge about Smurf books and related products from their lives as television viewers, supermarket shoppers and readers of mass-market texts. For example:

O'BRIEN: Can I hear from somebody who can tell us what they said in their group? What do you think she will do in this story? . . . Okay Jane, what will she do?

JANE: She is going up to the moon.

O'BRIEN: Uhm, what gave you that idea?

JONATHON: Because of the love hearts around that boy.

O'BRIEN: Rhianna

RHIANNA: That she'll live in a mushroom.

O'BRIEN: And how do you know that?

RHIANNA: (inaudible)

O'BRIEN: So Smurfs live in mushrooms, do they?

STUDENTS: Mushroom houses.

O'BRIEN: I'm sure they do. I've never read a Smurf book before. I've seen the covers but I've never really looked inside them.

(hubbub)

BEN: . . . on the TV in the morning . . .

(hubbub)

The 'hubbub' in this transcript indicates that this discussion has unleashed a number of small break-out conversations between students. Positioning myself as the inquirer, I acknowledge the limited part that Smurf books have played in my life, then draw on the children's greater knowledge by positioning them as the knowers who are able to use insights from their lives outside school to contribute to the discussion. When I admit that I haven't read a book or seen a program, students fill me in on the world of Smurfs, with many of them drawing on their own particular knowledge of Smurfs garnered from books and television.

My questions and remarks take for granted the children's access to the world of Smurfs. At this point, I could raise the possibility that some class members might belong to social groups whose reading practices don't include Smurfs. A series of questions focusing on the possibility that some children wouldn't be familiar with these works would direct the discussion towards uneven encounters with books and television programs. Diverse reading encounters children might have and the difference these might make to children's in- and out-of-school experiences can be an important element in text-based discussions. However, I don't take up this option this time. Instead, guided by my interest in unpicking some of the Smurf world view about gendered relations, I return to a comment made by one of the children.

O'BRIEN: Okay, someone said, Jonathon, you said something about the love hearts. Would you say what you wanted to say about that, please?

JONATHON: The girl is mad because he falls in love with her.

O'BRIEN: You think she, do you mean angry, she's angry because he falls in love. That's what she does . . .

ANTHEA: She doesn't want to.

O'BRIEN: Jonathon, why do you say that?

JONATHON: Because I can see the love hearts around her.

O'BRIEN: Because he's in love with her, it'll make her angry? Is that right?

JONATHON: Yes, because I can see her face.

O'BRIEN: Ah, so you're going by the look on her face in that picture . . . What do you think the writer won't tell you about her? Kayla?

KAYLA: Won't tell you how old she is

O'BRIEN: Why do you think that? . . . (pause) Anthea what do you think?

ANTHEA: They won't tell you if she has a real name or not.

O'BRIEN: How do you mean a *real name*?

ANTHEA: Because the name that she's going by in the story might not be her real name. 'Smurfette', it might not be her real name.

Lacking knowledge of the world of Smurfs, I encourage the children to take an expert role in describing what goes on in this world and how characters are represented. I ask questions that get children examining the text and what they already know about the text. I am keen to understand exactly what I'm being told, so I question the children closely and listen carefully to their revelations about how these texts work.

As the discussion progresses, I ask children to make guesses about the book based on the cover illustrations, their knowledge of gendered roles, and their knowledge of what writers might do with female characters. In the ensuing discussion, when children speculate about the aspects of the female Smurf's life that will not be revealed to them, they read and make predictions about this text in the light of their experiences with other Smurf texts. We continue our discussion and I position myself as the beginner among experts. I don't quite understand the point about Smurfette not having a real name but later this issue is raised again.

> O'BRIEN: Is that what you mean you won't find out her proper name? She'll just be called 'Smurfette' all the way through?
>
> ANTHEA: Yes.
>
> O'BRIEN: Isn't that interesting? Do the others have proper names or they all called Smurf, and Smurf, and Smurf?
>
> (Together, a number of students recite the names of the male characters.)

The students and I are operating on a number of 'levels' now. I don't know the range of possibilities or the history of these characters which the children know from their television experiences of Smurfs, so in response to my queries about the names of the male Smurfs, students draw on their specific textual knowledge to fill me in. In the subsequent discussion it emerges that the male characters have specific names, such as Hefty Smurf and Jokey Smurf, but the Smurfette is simply called 'Smurfette'.

It's now time to get into the narrative. I read the book aloud to my students and involve them in this reading as code breakers and text participants (see Luke and Freebody 1997). I direct children's attention to the 'commonsense' portrayal of male and female relations operating in this text by initiating discussion that questions the male domination which is taken for granted in the world of the Smurfs. As I read, I continue to share my unfamiliarity with Smurfs and their doings and invite children to explain them to me. At the same time, I make space for children to volunteer information and comments about aspects of the text that catch their interest:

> O'BRIEN: So, you people know quite a lot about Smurfs, or so I gather, and I know absolutely nothing. (continues reading)
>
> STUDENT: (loud snigger of anticipation)
>
> O'BRIEN: Something good coming?
>
> ALEX: (inaudible) . . . but the second bit's really funny.
>
> and a short time later:
>
> O'BRIEN: Is it? He misses? He jumps over the top of the moon? No? You're not going to tell me. (continues reading) This reminds me a bit of a fairy story where people, where men have to go out and do wonderful deeds to win the heart of the princess.

In this transcript segment, the children's laughter makes it clear that they anticipate something funny. I miss the humour, however, and can't predict what will happen as well as they can, so once more they are positioned as specialists in relation to this text. I decide to let go the question of what's funny, and with a reference to conventional fairy stories, I turn the talk to male–female relations in texts written for young children . . . and, at the same time, to male–female relations in the social world I share with these children.

My next move is to invite students to negotiate textual meaning as I come to an aspect of the narrative that surprises me: namely, repeated references to Smurfette getting married that don't seem to have their source in the plot of this text. I am uneasily aware that *A Lady in Smurfland* disrupts the expectations of textual logic that my career as a reader has prepared me for. I find, as I might have guessed, that my students are not particularly fazed by these references. I draw their attention to my puzzlement and seek their expert input:

> O'BRIEN: (continues reading) Is there something I should know that I don't know?
>
> STUDENT: (inaudible)
>
> O'BRIEN: So, there's something that would happen before this one, is there, Virginia? That I need to know? Can you explain what it is? You need to sit still. Everyone does.
>
> ANTHEA: She might be already married.
>
> O'BRIEN: But she said *'Don't you think it would be fun for me to get married?'*
>
> VIRGINIA: (inaudible)
>
> O'BRIEN: Oh, I see, and so you think if I'd read *Smurf Cake* I might know what is going on in *Lady in Smurfland*. Because I was very surprised about all that talk about being married. It just seemed to come out of the blue. (hubbub) Do you think that for me to understand this book I need to know more about Smurfs than I do?
>
> CHORUS: Ye-e-es.
>
> O'BRIEN: Are you surprised that all these people want to marry this girl?
>
> (hubbub)

Again, the room is buzzing with small conversations. As the talk continues, the children take up various stances in relation to the text and its meaning(s), and move in and out of roles that defend or explain the text. While I am learning from students about themes and interconnections among Smurf titles, I help them to re-read their knowledge of the world of Smurfs and to notice the ways in which male and female genders are represented in this popular book and television world. For example:

O'BRIEN:	Why's this surprising to you? . . . Kellie? Are you surprised that all these people want to marry this Smurfette?
KELLIE:	It's like that in most stories.
O'BRIEN:	How do you mean?
KELLIE:	This pretty girl comes along and all the boys want to marry her.
O'BRIEN:	I wonder why? What do you think?
ANTHEA:	Because she's the prettiest.
O'BRIEN:	What happens if you're not pretty? Do you have any chance of getting married?
CHORUS:	No-o.
O'BRIEN:	You look around the world. It's full of very ordinary looking people who get married. (laughs)

As I guide the talk towards the ways in which life options like marriage are represented in *A Lady in Smurfland*, I realise that for at least some of the children, the boundaries between life in books and life as they understand it are blurred. With my observation that 'ordinary looking people' get married, I make an effort to draw students' attention to the fact that the ideas and assumptions found in texts do not always correspond directly with real-life events and practices.

Interruptions to the flow of the narrative, like the one above, operate in at least three ways. First, they disrupt ideas of reading-aloud sessions as primarily entertainment or relaxation, or a time for a free-for-all of random response. Second, by drawing attention to *my* readings of the text, these interruptions work at de-naturalising children's readings and constructing new meanings for them to choose from. Third, interrupting 'conventional' narratives helps to get in the way of some 'commonsense' understandings of male–female relations in textual worlds as well as in students' everyday lives. This chapter presents just some of the questioning techniques and discussion points I use with my students to interrupt conventional readings and to begin 're-writing' these readings through our classroom talk.

Further discussion

A recent requirement of students in Australian schools is that they take a critical approach to classroom texts (*A Statement on English for Australian Schools* 1994). A reading lesson on texts like *A Lady in Smurfland* makes it possible for children to participate in a classroom discourse that includes a critical perspective on texts regardless of their literacy accomplishments or familiarity with official classroom talk and texts. Their admission ticket into this kind of discourse is the cultural capital they bring with them to school (Carrington and Luke 1996). In this particular case, these young students have a great deal of what is needed to join in the discussion of Smurf texts which are, after all, texts from their social worlds about which they have an elaborate store of understandings.

In my classroom, individual student knowledge about the Smurfs links with other sets of textual practices, (including my discourse of critical inquiry) and produces different readings of *A Lady in Smurfland*. Incorporating texts from children's lives and building lessons around their expertise makes it easier for children to participate in classroom-based reading lessons (that otherwise often come ready-scripted by means of conventional ways of 'doing school' and 'doing reading-aloud sessions'), while at the same time expanding their ability to analyse and question the authorised discourses of texts and the talk that goes on around them in class.

Giving Smurf books and children's rich understandings of them a place in classrooms—not just putting up with them, not ignoring them, not finding fault with them, but treating them seriously—has several benefits. First, they offer a useful departure point for examining 'commonsense' representations of males and females in books and in everyday life. Second, by weaving texts of commercial culture into the rich fabric of classroom talking, reading and writing practices, teachers help to make connections between students' lives in school and out of school. Third, teachers can view children's understandings about these texts as rich literate resources that have the potential—if taken up meaningfully in classrooms—to set them off along one of many possible pathways to success in reading (Dyson 1993).

Looking ahead

I'm committed to putting texts up for scrutiny and questioning. Ultimately, I aim at producing flexible readers who are able to read one text in many ways, ask different kinds of questions about texts, and make an assessment about how different readings will position them in different circumstances. This chapter has presented one of the ways in which I begin this work.

The critical position I claim is based on the understanding that the content of texts that children read *does* matter; that as children learn to read they can also learn to read the world and versions of their roles in the world and learn to understand how texts work *on them*. I never assume that this sort of language work is too hard or that children won't enjoy it; it isn't and they do.

NOTE

I would like to acknowledge that this discussion of the *A Lady in Smurfland* transcript draws extensively on work done by Barbara Comber generously shared with me.

References

A Statement on English for Australian schools: A Joint Project of the States, Territories and the Commonwealth of Australia initiated by the Australian Education Council (1994). Carlton, Victoria: Curriculum Corporation.

Carrington, V and Luke, A (1997) 'Literacy and Bourdieu's sociological theory: A reframing', *Language and Education* Vol 11 No 2 pp. 96–112.

Dyson, A (1992) 'Whistle for Willie lost puppies, and cartoon dogs: The sociocultural dimensions of young children's composing', *Journal of Reading Behaviour.* Vol XXIV, No 4, pp 432–462.

Dyson, A (1993) 'From invention to social action in early childhood literacy: A reconceptualisation through dialogue about difference', *Early Childhood Research Quarterly.* December.

Dyson, A (1995) 'The courage to write: Child meaning making in a contested world', *Language Arts.* Vol 72, No 5, September.

Luke, A (1993) 'The social construction of literacy in the primary school', in *Literacy learning and teaching: Language as social practice in the primary school.* Edited by Len Unsworth. Melbourne: Macmillan.

Luke, A (1995) 'The social practice of reading'. Conference paper delivered at the Australian Reading Association Twenty-first National Conference. Darling Harbour, Sydney, 12–15 July 1995.

Luke, A and Freebody, P (1997) 'The social practices of reading'. In S Muspratt, A Luke and P Freebody (eds) *Constructing Critical Literacies.* Cresskill, New Jersey: Hampton Press.

Peyo (n.d.) *A Lady in Smurfland* (no publication information).

CHAPTER 3

The Woody Kids

ANNAH HEALY

In this chapter, Annah Healy reports the everyday literacy practices she observed in one classroom over a two-year period. The focus is on one teacher and her negotiable pact with students to engage in rich literacy events in contexts where an unambiguous commitment is made to real-life language and literacy practices. The potential power of language and its relationship to the students' lives is core business for this teacher.

The site and the classroom community

The school to which this group of students belong is sited in a large Housing Commission area on the outskirts of one of Australia's smallest cities. For the first few years in the life of this school, buildings and grounds were vandalised regularly. Warfare wounds are now duly licked and healed, and the climate in the school and the community spirit surrounding it, altogether changed. Much of the turnaround is due to the dedicated work of a group of educators who acknowledge in their daily operations the social and cultural climates which surround their students' life worlds and which have framed these students' language uses.

It is not my purpose here to describe the events which changed a war zone into a community place. Suffice to say that the one-time staffroom is now a communal centre where students, teachers, parents, carers and older siblings alike engage in a variety of activities. The school complex includes a day-care 'respite' centre, and an art resource room also serves as an adult literacy centre staffed by volunteer parents and three retired teachers. In every sense of the word, there is an organic community at work here.

The school community is subdivided into family groups each of which are referred to by an Aboriginal name significant to the local region. However, the group around which this chapter revolves is referred to by the title they give themselves: 'The Woody Kids'. Twenty-seven students comprise the group, three of them are only eight years in age, and each has an older sibling in the same group. The remainder of the students range in age from nine to eleven years. Meg is their teacher. Teachers like Meg pioneer ways of working with students in present times when a relevant curriculum in response to a changing literacy is an amoebaean form, and where communications fluctuate between the products of a print world and cyberspace. Day-to-day literacy practices in the classroom shift between familiar and unfamiliar landscapes, organised around an unshakeable belief in the worth of helping students go beyond what they know, to see what is possible for them. Language, in this sense, is respected as having a potential power by which individuals can learn to manage their participation in life.

Providing a context for the events reported here requires some explanation of the particular view of literacy in operation in Meg's classroom. The propositions for *critical* language awareness put forward by Lankshear (1996), Wallace (1992) and Fairclough (1992) for example, where scrutiny of texts and Discourses (Gee, 1992) are intrinsic to establishing meaning, are embedded in, and constitutive of, daily practice for Meg and her students. She describes the curriculum she plans with her students as a problem-solving one where acts of writing and talking have a volatile, fluid state, and become the connective tissue in students' explorations of matter and relationships between matter. Connections are made between what children write and talk about, and what they have read and viewed as they establish different views of the world.

Being critically literate certainly isn't seen as any finite state. Meg's ways of operating 'critically' are made transparent through Colin Lankshear's view of critical literacy. He points out that a sociocultural approach to language and literacy is 'committed not only to situating people and texts in coordinations, trajectories and Discourses, but to a certain sort of what we might call . . . 'critical literacy' . . . [which] arises from the very nature of elements-in-coordinations-in Discourses' (1997: xvii). Indeed, all texts are acted upon by history and by socially constructed meanings. Thus, in terms of the learners' processes, self-direction, interrogation, accuracy and practical application are only *aspects* of a critical approach to literacy. A key condition for critical literacy practice is where decisions about use and interpretation are made on the understanding that elements of language carry different meanings and effects for different groups of people in different contexts.

At the beginning of each school term, Meg and the Woody Kids together plan for guests to come to their learning site as contributors to special projects. Parents and carers involved in the daily life of the school join in when invited. This classroom is very much a community of people in which teacher and students co-decide their *modus operandi*. Literacy-based events in and around this classroom are each choreographed to enable students to learn something more about their world and to explore myriad ways of operating in it. Tasks are inextricably bound up with the production of texts, arguments about text, and analysis and critique of the reproduction and maintenance of unequal social relationships through language use.

There are no special times set aside for literacy in this classroom and there are few demarcations between the curriculum areas. Reading, writing and talk rarely have scheduled beginning or end points in the sense that some classrooms have special times set aside for children to read or to write.

The students, including the eight-year-olds in the group, are provided with opportunities to strengthen their authority as writers and analysts of texts and situations, and to collaborate and negotiate in their social groups. Meg knows that the children learn as much from each other as they do from her. Her students become adept at communicating for a range of purposes, and view their activities in terms of goals to be met and texts to be produced. At the same time as the students prepare to construct their own texts, they critically analyse the texts of others in terms of author position, their bias/truth and target audience. Projects can be an hour long or take several weeks to complete, but importantly, the students see the *purpose* for adopting roles of code breaker, text participant, user and analyst (Freebody and Luke, 1990) according to the task in hand. Meg bases lessons in real-life and life-like practices. Indeed, the organising principle behind her curriculum is one of purpose. Visitors to the group comment on the ability of the children to articulate the problems they encounter *en route* through a task, and their independence in getting assistance. There is no organised system of peer tutoring as such, but students freely assist each other on a needs basis.

One chapter is insufficient to track the daily events of this class or to do justice to the inspiration of one teacher who believes her major responsibility is to prepare her students as best she can, for a changing world. It would not work particularly well in this instance to provide a linear description of any single event to capture the strength of Meg's curriculum as the 'flavour' of the group would be lost. Instead, five specific events have been selected to report, in mostly narrative form. Although each of these events has its own shape and potential in a critical literacy context.

GREAT-GRANDMA NELLY
The critical focus

The way in which projects in this classroom find their way into others, and how issues are taken up over and again in different guises and from different viewpoints, provides Meg with a natural vehicle for exploring phenomena. As in life, closure to one event can be a springboard to another. From Meg's point of view, her focus during the project was on texts and their ideologies, and on ways of having students explore texts to show their 'constructedness' and intended audiences. More broadly speaking, Meg's goals in projects such as this are to go beyond the nature of a particular text and how it is used, to provide students with a meta-perspective on the social and cultural practices surrounding the texts. Students are learning to put together the crucial resources for critiquing social practices through the texts produced by the local and wider community, and to go about strategically achieving goals through learning how to critique and construct texts for particular contexts. Exploration of a text's ideology is daily practice in Meg's classroom, and the Woody Kids are able to engage with fictional and pragmatic worlds in balance. One of the truly remarkable features of the classroom is that, given that the students are very familiar with popular culture texts, there is little parody evident in their own.

THE STARTING POINT

Paul is nine years old and lives sometimes with his mother and four other children and, at other times, with his great-grandmother, Nelly, who lives alone in the next street. Nelly works in the tuckshop at the school and is a frequent visitor to the classroom where she sometimes helps out. Nelly arrives one Monday morning with a shoe box full of old greeting cards, some of which are dated prior to the Second World War. She explains to Meg that the pictures might be 'good for something or other in the classroom'.

THE ACTION

At the end of that day Meg discusses the purpose of greeting cards as a form of social communication. Some of the most interesting cards from Nelly's collection are displayed, and Meg provides a couple of card-related anecdotes and invites children to contribute their own. She explores with the children the notion of change in social communications. The discussion goes beyond the purpose of greeting cards, and Meg uses the opportunity to focus on changes to life in Australia over the last fifty years. The children decide that they should interview Nelly to find out what life was like during the 1930s, and what changes she has witnessed.

There is now an invitation to be written to Nelly and interview questions to be formulated. Ten-year-old Amanda suggests that there ought to be some organisation in the interview to avoid having a question posed more than once, so decisions are made about setting up question categories. It is decided by the children that the focus areas would be *'communication when Nelly was young'*, *'entertainment at home before TV, video and computer games'*. Eight-year-old Danny wants to ask why old people keep 'all that stuff' for so long, but it is explained to him by eleven-year-old Sarah that his question isn't a category, and can be asked as part of the 'communication' section. It is decided that Nelly should be given an afternoon tea for her efforts, so the children seek help from some of the parents who regularly attend the school.

The children's responsibilities are co-decided. Three of the older children have the responsibility for costing out the makings of a simple afternoon tea. Cross-aged groups are formed to compose questions, and on Saul's suggestion, it is agreed that there should be no more than ten questions to ensure that Nelly 'doesn't get tired of answering'. Ten-year-old Steven thinks it sensible if the questions are recorded on the computer, to allow others to see them and make comments before Nelly's interview. It is decided that a review of the questions would be a good idea. Eight-year-old twins, Cindy and Simone, announce that they will dress up like reporters to ask their questions. The suggestion stimulates Sandra to suggest that different perspectives are taken for the interviewing process, to make it more interesting for them and for Nelly. Decisions are made for adopting roles as media reporters, as historians, and as writers seeking material for a novel or picture book. This involves critical examination of the texts of others and their language uses, and students deciding with their teacher which are exemplar models on which to base their own. Operations thus far are viewed by Meg as a beginning point from which strategies will be chosen to conduct several versions of an interview.

A crucial second stage is planned by Meg to help students hone their questions to be more specific and to introduce the notion of expectations accorded to, and stereotypical views of, the roles played by men and women in various occupations over the years. Meg works with the students to moderate their existing questions in order to enable students to gain a view of the social dynamics existing at the time when Nelly was young and 'courting'.

Following a successful interview session with Nelly, her responses are taken up for the purpose of exploring stereotypical patterns of behaviour within families. Anthony Browne's *Piggy Book* is used as a specific starting point.

At the same time that Nelly's interview is being set up, the Woody Kids are considering how to raise the money needed for taking an overnight excursion as part of a near-future project. Meg explores with the children ways of using the information they gained from Nelly's interview to entertain others. It is agreed that the class will construct a series of three shadow-puppet plays. The Woody Kids are now obliged to construct texts for presenting their ideas, make their shadow puppets, explore the potential of sound effects, and to advertise the event. Permission has to be gained from the Principal, so nine-year-old Megan and Alicia write an explanatory letter which also seeks permission to proceed. As a class, the students decide to ask the principal for advice on a charge rate.

With permission in place, it is agreed that a poster advertising the performances will go out to the rest of the school, and local shopkeepers will be approached to place an advertisement in their windows. Parents and friends are also to be invited. The group decides that Nelly should be asked to be the MC, and set about inviting her to participate in their performance.

GARDENING

The critical focus

Critical literacy is more than critique of social and cultural texts; it is also about affecting change in one's environment through literacy acts. The implications of the current changing nature of our textual environment, and changes in the types of work done by the community make demands on literacy greater than they have probably ever been. Not only do students have to understand the different interactional codes in operation, they also have to translate from one code to another and to mix the codes for effective communication.

The meaningfulness of the gardening project is reflected in students' genuine understanding of how to achieve what is, to all intents and purposes, an overwhelming, often prohibitive task; that is, making sense of the inseparable nature of learning, literacy and the world (Freire and Macedo 1987). The students' immersion in a community project, which they were effectively directing, involved the critical thinking skills of decision making, comparing and contrasting, and orchestrating complex sequences of events in a meaningful, real-world context. In addition, this project entailed students coming to grips with the role of institutions in making projects possible (or impossible). Such a practice is a long way from children 'doing a project' on rainforests within the boundaries of the four walls of the classroom! Here there is purpose for literacy learning associated with real-life: constructing formal letters, making phone calls, using fax machines, utilising the Internet to search out information, and for presenting a case.

THE STARTING POINT

The classroom has two sets of doors, one which leads out to an uninteresting asphalt corner which no-one ever uses. The area was once planted up, but the site is devoid of any sign of life. The children have been learning about the importance of rainforests around the world through a variety of media including CD ROM. As part of that project, a prominent TV celebrity gardener, Peter the Gardener, was invited to the classroom to talk to the children about trees and the importance of green belts in and around cities. During one of his three visits, the class took a walk with him around the school grounds. With notebooks in hand, they were shown how to map areas according to north–south directionality, and various suggestions were made for a possible replanting program in the school grounds.

THE ACTION

Children set about analysing the information they had been provided with or collected, with the aim of establishing priority areas in the grounds for replanting, categorising fast-growing and slow-growing trees and shrubs, and establishing watering demands and sun direction in relation to the siting of various plants. Students learned about shadow sticks at this point, as they needed to check sun and shadow patterns for planting purposes. Four shadow sticks were placed at strategic points around the building and over one school day in winter, the children registered the sun and shadow patterns. Meg took this opportunity to explore the notion that these patterns would change with the different seasons, and children were asked many questions to which they had to come up with possible answers from investigating texts that described the rotation of suns and planets and their effects on the seasons. A joint decision was made that the group would plan for a long-term planting project, beginning with one for planting up the area immediately outside their classroom as soon as possible.

Meg and her students jointly construct a letter to the Principal and the Parents and Friends (P&F) group for their next meeting, the subject of which is a proposal for the regeneration of the school grounds as a 'mini park'. The letter is accompanied by six possible plans which had taken groups up to two weeks of concentrated effort to complete.

Stage 1 of the plan involves running a competition in which the population of the school, including parents and visitors, will be asked to cast a vote on the mini park plans. Display boards are organised with the help of the teacher-librarian in an open space in the library, and the children explore ways of exhibiting their work. Decisions are made on time-lines and about collecting the votes, and nine-year-old Marcia thinks it is very important to include information about the project and what it involves with the exhibit. Marcia had seen a display of a future council project in the local shopping centre which included such details. Other notices are placed around the school encouraging children to visit the display and cast their votes.

A two-week limit was decided on for casting votes, and Saul is nominated to advertise the competition over the PA system immediately before a lunch break. At every spare moment the two weeks are taken up in planning the operation. A letter is sent to the State Forestry Commission seeking prices for the trees and shrubs suggested by their horticulturist friend Peter, and the group decide to present the project at the next P&F meeting with the hope of receiving a donation toward their project. Eleven-year-old Damian is elected by the group to present the proposal which involves a poster display and verbal report of the action so far. Additionally, Damian is to ask for commitments for volunteer labour for planting. Ten-year-old Stevie thinks it's not a good idea to rely on attendance at the meeting to secure the level of help that will be needed, providing the example of his own dad who never attends the meetings, but who Stevie is certain will help out. So, a second explanatory outline of the project, its aims and requirements is constructed. This goes home with one child from each family attending the school. Two children construct a letter to the managers of the two local supermarkets, providing a plan of the project, and a request for either plant or financial donations.

The realities of the cost of such a project emerge. However, the Woody Kids are encouraged by a letter from the Forestry Commission promising 50 free plants for every 200 purchased, and a donation of one giant oak as a 'specimen tree'. Children have the opportunity to explore the nature of the language used in the pamphlets and letter, as well as the workings of 'retail' and 'wholesale' prices and outlets and their role in the commercial world. The classroom is flooded with charts, sketches and diagrams, and written information on various aspects of landscaping. Through CD ROMs and print texts students learn about such things as 'companion planting' and 'natural wind-breaks'. Simon enters the classroom one morning very excited because a tree type he had read about the day before, described as the 'oldest living tree specimen on earth', exists in a garden across the road from the school. Meg notes that the children pay more attention to their surroundings since the project began, and that during one 'block walk' which the class had taken to look for suitable specimens for their own project, informed discussions about 'natives' and 'exotics' were happening.

Peter the Gardener has commitments interstate and cannot offer any further support to the project, but on his suggestion, a phone call to the Forestry Commission Plant Nursery secured the services of Max who agrees to assist in matters of soil preparation and grouping shrubs and trees to help their survival. Interestingly, Max suggests planting up the area outside the classroom as a miniature rainforest, the subject which had begun the group's interest in the first place.

The competition is judged, the P&F and a local community business group each donate money toward the project; the school is given an assistance grant from the Education Department. The Woody Kids' Mini Park Project is alive and well.

Three years later, five of the eight stages of the project are completed. The classroom is no longer occupied by Meg and the Woody Kids, but their heritage is in the form of a still immature, but fast-growing miniature rainforest, through which a woodchip path snakes its way to a seat where current students go to read, talk, or engage in other projects.

TAKING CARE OF FRED
The critical focus

There are many aspects to critical language awareness, and learning to adapt, change and learn skills relevant to the times is about entering 'discourse' and 'Discourse' (Gee 1992) in a 'learning enterprise [which] is strategically crucial' (Perelman 1992). Lifelong learning is established only through practices which can be extrapolated to other situations, and as a result of an ability to critique the worthiness of texts in relation to their contexts. The diaries students constructed while caring for Fred (a two-week-old black sheep) capture more than feeding times and notes about Fred's physical characteristics. Meg had many opportunities to explore with the group their use of language and how words mean different things to different people. Arguments about words and their meanings generated discussion about social beliefs, and opened doors to explorations of cultural practices and how these bear on what people believe, how they act, and therefore how they compose texts. Meg focused considerably on verbal texts during this project in exploring students' conceptions of family and so on. For example, the feeding of Fred raised questions about masculine–feminine roles and parenting which Meg took up as an ideological discussion. Particular videos were employed for students to explore and then analyse the relationships between characters. Changes to children's stereotypes of families, the roles and relationships played out in family, and many other fruitful discussions emerged from 'managing Fred'.

THE STARTING POINT

Fred has been abandoned by his mother, and (with permission granted on all sides) is brought to school by Simon who is eight years old, and his sister Claudia who is just ten. The children are armed with bottles and a milk supply, and their dad has a disused child's playpen and a bag of straw in tow. At first, the pen is placed inside the classroom and bedded with straw. If no major dramas arise, it is agreed that Fred will come to school each day for a month.

Meg has noted that very few members of her class have a pet and she would like the students to consider the notion of responsibility in moral and practical terms. Meg makes one of very few executive decisions. She decides on the constitution of the group who will be responsible for Fred's care. While any one of the students is free to fondle and talk to Fred, six of the younger children, none of whom have a pet at home, are nominated as Fred's carers. The group is advised that at the end of the month, each of them will have written their personal observations of taking care of a relatively vulnerable creature.

THE ACTION

On advice from Claudia, Fred has to be fed with the bottle each hour, and his pen kept clean. The carer group decide that a note diary is a good idea for keeping a record of the times when Fred is fed, and also to record the volume of milk Fred drinks at each session, and over the month. There is considerable debate about who is to do which task. Nicola determines that the only fair option is for the group to divide into two, and on an alternate basis, one trio will share the feeding and record those details, while the other takes responsibility for keeping Fred's pen clean.

Meg asks the group to make a list of anything they will need, and reminds them to think of hygiene factors as part of this task. Stephanie has drawn a diagram of the area and the children have labelled it to show that they will need a supply of newspaper, two bowls (one for water inside the pen, and the other with soap for students to wash their hands) to be placed near the pen, a plastic bag and a dustpan. Stephanie makes the suggestion that the note diary should not only have spaces for the dates and times and for recording details about Fred, but also a space where comments can be written about him. The children question whether Fred will need to drink water in addition to milk, but neither Simon nor Claudia are certain. The children make a decision that it is better that the option is made available to Fred. Stephanie gets worried on Day 2 that Fred has had no time in the direct sun. After morning play-break, Fred's pen is placed in view of the classroom outside on a grassy area. Melanie writes a sign for the pen 'PLEASE LET FRED HAVE HIS SLEEPS' when she becomes concerned that the lamb is receiving almost constant attention from other students as they move about the school in the normal course of their work.

The group visit the library to find out what they can about pet care and various texts are brought back to the classroom for reference. By the second week, the two students in the group who couldn't tell time from an analogue clock have learned to do so from keeping their schedules, and from having to set the alarm for feedings. Meg has the opportunity to discuss with the children the phenomenon of white ewes sometimes abandoning their black offspring, which brings up other subjects including animals and their restricted colour sight. Sayings such as 'red rag to a bull' are explored for their accuracy, and the children set about searching out other sayings in common usage and their heritage.

At the end of a month caring for Fred, and a few minor dramas later, the group and other members of the class have discussed and written about him a good deal. One word-processed picture book and its handcrafted paintings describing the adventures of *Lucy the Lamb in Space* is read to the entire school at a Friday assembly and with permission from its author, eleven-year-old Lucy, is officially catalogued into the library for other children to access. Fred's diary runs to 16 double pages, and includes a record of his milk consumption, a plethora of facts about pet care, statements, observations and one poem entered by nine-year-old Troy who takes every opportunity to be at Fred's pen:

> I don't know what enters Freds head
> it could be his dreams or about his mum
> which makes him sad until we say his name
> and give him his milk or put him in the sun
> you think when you cuddle him that he'll be very soft
> but he's quite brissly [sic] and his tummy is hot.

THE SUPPORT GROUP

Note: The support group is reported differently from other events on the basis that a brief background is essential for explicating its unique purpose, and because certain aspects are collated—brought together from different times—and reported by several observers.

The critical focus

It is argued by some that in the absence of any conscious effort on the teacher's part to incorporate into class contexts discourse of the type recorded in the event which follows, students will find their own opportunities to talk about each other's problems anyway—and of course they will. However, the critical literacy at work in these sessions bears little relationship to the chat in which children engage during everyday, informal social activity. Notions of 'practical activities in oral language' of the type where 'talk' is taken up as something to be developed in and of itself has no relationship to the dialogue at work in the support group. Meg approaches talk as a powerful text, and critique is structured around the networks of communication that impact on students personally. There is a belief operating here that critiquing spoken text is as important as critiquing written texts. The structure in place in the support group sessions provides for ways of examining cause and effect, problem and solution, and opportunities are generated for speakers and listeners to measure the relevance of each possible solution. Talk is about exploring myriad ways of dealing with life's experiences in a supportive context.

THE SETTING

Twice a week, or as need demands, the Woody Kids leave the classroom to go to an indoor drama studio for a discussion session. There is carpet on the floor but little else in the space. In these sessions, Meg considers it important for the children to be removed from their familiar classroom space to one less personal to them.

THE PURPOSE

The purpose of the support group is for the children to discuss issues which are personally meaningful to them. The discussion topics include personal problems encountered outside the school, social problems within and outside the class, and difficulties experienced with aspects of their work. The code of conduct encouraged here includes demonstration of respect for one another and each other's ideas and problems, and that support group discussions are 'closed circuits' of communication.

THE DYNAMICS

At the beginning of each year the class is provided with a clear framework of operation for supporting each other in these peer-support sessions. Each student takes a pad and pencil to the sessions and a yellow card which will secure their right to respond to other members during discussions. The children who wish to open a discussion or raise an issue take a blue card. The children form a circle and someone elects to open the discussion.

Meg does not join the circle, but sits on the floor outside it. She reasons that the cards maintain order and help keep her out of the discussions as much as possible. The card system prevails until such time as the children respect the protocols involved and demonstrate that they can operate without them. Only one person is permitted to speak at a time, and it is up to a blue card holder to invite responses from those holding up yellow cards. Students are reminded that the pad is for jotting down notes or questions as a memory aid in case there is no immediate opportunity given for their response. When responses have finished, a self-appointed student concludes each 'blue card' segment, and asks the blue card holder if any of the suggestions have been helpful. Students are also required to articulate any decisions made on taking action in response to the problem or question.

AN EXAMPLE
Donna's problem
Donna joined the Woody Kids six weeks prior to her taking her first blue card to the session. She had been noted to be attentive in other sessions and in the previous one, had jotted down some notes and held up a yellow card in response to a problem about being bullied on the way to school, but had not been invited to speak at that session.

Donna (10 years):	I get really scared in maths sometimes—I don't—know—um—work out how to do some of it—'n I get really embarrassed—cos—everyone else is going away there—you know chattin' about stuff—'n doin' it—'n I get worried about it—I used to do it okay—at me last school'n that—

Three responses

Rebekkah (11 years):	Um—everyone finds something hard at times—you know—you mighn't have understood the problem—or you're having a bad day—or something else is on your mind—you know—but I know that sometimes lots o' kids find *maths* hard—sometimes writing is hard—but maths you get sorta right—or wrong—so people worry about it—but I think you could concentrate on the *first* part o' the—problem—the bit that first stops you—'n ask someone to explain it to ya—or go to the teacher—'n say—'I don't understand this'—'cos if you go on not sayin' *anything*—you'll get further behind—
Cindy (8 years):	When I find anything—really hard—I ask me big brother—he's Saul [she points]—'n sometimes he says—so 'n so is better than me—go and ask her—but—*someone* will help ya—
Damian (11 years):	Ah—the thing is—you shouldn't get someone just to do it for ya—that's not gonna help—I reckon it'd be a good idea—if—um—people volunteered—their names on the board'd be best—like each week—we could have a roster or somethin'—'n then if the teacher's busy—anyone on the board'd do—sometimes—like on Monday—when we had an editor circle—someone gave me this really good idea—it could be the same in maths—but ya gotta ask the questions—

Donna likes the sound of having a list of possible helpers and agrees to identify what it is that she doesn't understand before seeking assistance. In terms of critical literacy, the support group discussions are not necessarily instances of critical literacy *per se*. Without a doubt, however, these discussions and enacted outcomes *do* contribute in a very real sense to these students beginning to see themselves as active 'agents of change', a key dimension of a full-blown critical literacy practice.

BREAKFAST

The critical focus

Developing capacities for reflecting on social practices is not as simple as it would seem. Students in Meg's class learn by means of the breakfast program to define their own needs in relation to others, and to cater for the needs of others within the constraints of, among other things, a financial budget. The processes involved in the program are considered as important by the parents and carers of these students as they are by Meg. One of the interesting elements evident from the relationships established between Meg and many of the adults in her students' lives is the clear message that they want better for their children than they have for themselves. In itself, this is not so remarkable. What is important is that they see the opportunities given to their children to prepare themselves for life in the wider community, and recognise the importance of the competencies their children exhibit.

Meg has a certain ambivalence toward 'counting' this program as part of her critical literacy agenda, especially when compared to other practices which have their feet more overtly planted in critique. But in many ways, at least from an observer's viewpoint, the adroit manner in which the Woody kids approach and deal with the day-to-day dilemmas that arise in the breakfast program, serves to epitomise the effectiveness of her critical literacy practices across the curriculum.

THE SITUATION

The school runs a breakfast program for children who choose not, or do not have the opportunity, to fuel themselves for the day. Not eating breakfast at home appears to happen for a number of reasons. As one example, some children enter the morning 'between parents', as many of their parents work shifts at one of a number of industrial sites within a 20-kilometre range of the suburb in which these children live. It seems that for a number of children, and in a regular cycle, one parent has left the home to take up a shift before the night-shift parent arrives home. While food may be available, the children don't always choose to eat without parental supervision. In addition, the social order in the community is diverse, and the daily lives of the families often marked by upheaval of one kind of another. Teachers have made a commonsense decision to ensure wherever possible that every child will begin their day with the kind of food that helps sustain active participation.

THE ACTION

Meg's class has opted to take responsibility for the breakfast program for the year. She sees it as an opportunity for her students to learn about budgeting, catering, regular participation in a responsible task which affects others, and the opportunity for children to monitor events over a long term. There are many minor benefits, and some major ones too.

The program involves keeping within a budget and estimating how many children will continue to pay the 50-cent fee. Recording how many children take advantage of the service over a two-week period, what they consume, and working on that average for the following fortnight is a major responsibility. Fruit, a milk drink, cereal, toast, muesli bars and a range of preserves are standard fare, but the children can make suggestions for other items to replace current ones. The children who participate in the breakfast program indicate each day what they ate, thus providing the caterers with a supply and demand balance on which to operate. It is not unusual for some parents to join the children at breakfast, some admitting a preference for being 'catered for'. The children decide that participating adults should pay $1 as many of them ask for tea or coffee in addition to food.

Meg's students are responsible for the blackboard display in the kitchen area where the children eat. They are free to create a menu, or to 'push' a special if they wish to clear some of the stock. Displays common to cafes have been studied by the children from a series of photographs taken around the city eateries at an earlier time.

Twice a week the 'duty' children have the responsibility for scouring the advertised 'specials' put out by the two competing supermarkets in the area. Lists are constructed in relation to the state of supplies, and costs estimated. The children have access to the 'banking' sheets and do the rosters for teachers, parents and children for duty over the two-week cycle. Achieving a smooth-running program involves a good deal of paperwork and organisation. Once children become adept themselves at handling the situation, they set about teaching others. Normally, two children have primary responsibility for the program with a team of six others rotating between the various duties over one month. There is a one-week 'hand-over' period for a different team to take charge. Everything is regularly recorded, and the 'books' become an official record of operations. Every once in a while the children brainstorm ideas for a special pancake morning or the like, and hold regular reviews of the program. The students understand that this is a non-profit program, but they also know that it cannot work as a deficit one, so take pride in keeping their books straight, and to work realistically.

Conclusion

The events recorded in this chapter are few of the many which could have been described. At the point when the final-year undergraduate Education students and I could no longer be engaged in Meg's classroom, the Woody Kids, under the guidance of Ted the Writer set out on a trail of 'people spotting'. In such projects student knowledge is built around real issues and practices, and their learning about language and literacy is linked elaborately to analysing events and situations as fluctuating forms. Perspectives are recognised by these students to be multiple and also to be respected. One of the most impressive elements which comes through in students' conversations concerns their understanding of themselves in relation to the realities of their environment. Meg ensures as much as possible that she provides for her students the flexible practices essential for a critical literacy and in so doing, helps them to write their own ticket for gaining access to a life in which they can be critical participants.

References

Freebody, P and Luke, A (1990) 'Literacies programs: Debates and demands in cultural contexts', *Prospect*. No 5, pp 7–16.

Freire, P and Macedo, D (1987) *Literacy: Reading the Word and the World*. South Hadley, Massachusetts: Bergin and Garvey.

Gee, J P (1992) *The Social Mind: Language Ideology and Social Practice*. New York: Bergin and Garvey.

Gee, J P (1993) 'Literacies: Tuning in to forms of life', *Education Australia*. No 19, pp 13–14.

Lankshear, C (1997) *Changing Literacies*, Philadelphia: Open University Press.

Luke, A (1993) 'The social construction of literacy in the primary school', in L Unsworth (ed) *Literacy Learning and Teaching: Language as Social Practice in the Primary School*. Melbourne: Macmillan.

Perelman, L (1992) *School's Out: The New Technology and the End of Education*. New York: Morrow.

Stanovich, K (1986) 'Matthew effects in reading: Some consequences of individual differences in the acquisition of literacy', *Reading Research Quarterly*. No 21, pp 360–407.

CHAPTER 4

A woman's place: a discussion of the place of linguistic analysis in critical literacy in the upper primary school

PETER WIGNELL

Peter Wignell emphasises the importance of a meta-level understanding of language in developing critical literacy skills and strategies. He provides the reader with two anecdotes about the telling ways in which one young girl demonstrates her knowledge of the ways in which language works. He then takes the lyrics from three popular songs and illustrates the use of simple, but effective, analytical tools that can be used by primary school students in the middle to upper grades. These tools are derived from systemic functional linguistics and are used to look at the ways in which language 'constructs' representations of males and females in popular songs.

My intention in this chapter is to demonstrate that a relatively small amount of explicit linguistic knowledge and a relatively small amount of language for talking about language and text can enhance the critical literacy and critical thinking skills of quite young children. This point is illustrated and developed first through two examples drawn from my personal experience and second through an analysis of three pop songs, using a very small number of analytical tools drived from systemic functional linguistics. I have 'read' the songs as different constructions of being female (and male) which demonstrate an evolution or change over two decades. What I have attempted to do in this chapter is integrate critical literacy practices into possible classroom activities so that the language work and the critical analysis are not seen as separate things, but rather as mutually reinforcing. The work presented in this chapter is designed to act as a model for teachers interested in using systemic functional linguistic analysis with students as a critical literacy 'tool'. Consequently, I have chosen songs that suit my present purposes (ie they interest teachers), and strongly suggest that teachers who plan to merge linguistic analysis and critical literacy will want to select songs that meet the interests of their students.

I will begin with the story of Sam. At the time of this incident Sam was nine years old and in Year 4 at a suburban Darwin primary school. The incident happened one evening when I was babysitting Sam and her sister. Sam's mother had put Sam to bed before she left and I settled in to watch a movie on television. I don't recall the name of the movie but it was a more or less standard 'disaster and rescue' narrative. A family in a small boat were shipwrecked in a storm in winter in, I think, Canada. The family survived catastrophe after catastrophe and false hope after false hope until finally they saved themselves.

Very soon after her mother had gone, Sam got herself out of bed and sat herself on the lounge to watch the movie with me. After about ten minutes Sam said: 'This is a narrative, you know.' I was surprised but didn't let on. I just said something like: 'Oh yeah, how do you know that?' Sam's analysis and my cross-examination went along the lines of:

SAM: Well, they've just had the oriatation [sic] and this is the complication now.

ME: What do you reckon's going to happen next?

SAM: Well, it should be the resolution but this kind of narrative's different.

ME: What do you mean?

SAM: Well, mostly in a narrative you get a oriatation [sic], a complication and a resolution but in this kind you think it's going to be a resolution but they have another complication, sometimes lots of complications before you get to the resolution.

ME: Why do you reckon they do that?

SAM: It kind of makes it more exciting because they trick you into thinking it's going to be the resolution but it isn't, so it's, like, more exciting.

ME: That all, you reckon?

SAM: And . . . it would be kind of boring if they just went to the resolution . . . and it wouldn't be very long so they wouldn't fill up enough time and they wouldn't be able to get many ads in . . .

After this discussion I asked Sam if I could see her schoolbook. I looked at her most recent work. The last two pages of writing came under the heading *Narratives*. Under the heading there was a photocopy of a short narrative stuck into the book. The story had been divided into sections with space left for writing a heading for each section. Sam had written *oriatation*, *complication* and *resolution* above the appropriate stages of the story. On the next page there was a photocopied sheet containing information about the functions of orientations, complications and resolutions in the structure of a narrative text. I asked Sam how long her class had been 'doing' narratives and she said that they had started them that week.

Several points emerge from this example. With a small amount of prompting I thought Sam produced a fairly sophisticated critical analysis for a nine-year-old. She had transferred knowledge about text in one medium, writing, to text presented in another medium, film. In doing this she had recognised similarities in the patterning of the texts. Perhaps more importantly, she had the rudiments of a vocabulary for talking about the texts: she had the beginnings of a language for talking about and analysing text. Even with this fairly minimal vocabulary—she knew four technical terms (*narrative*, *'oriatation'*, *complication*, *resolution*)—she was able to talk about similar texts in two different media, make observations about variations in how texts develop and make some observations on the social context of the movie (ie getting the ads in). I suggest that Sam's ability to deliver this analysis of the movie was greatly enhanced by the small amount of technical knowledge she had and would have been greatly reduced if she had not had this knowledge.

My second example of critical literacy skills and primary school children also involves Sam, this time she is two years older and in year six. Sam was about to go to bed when the beginnings of the Sunday night movie came on the screen. The movie was *Fatal Attraction*. Sam stopped and watched the screen. The 'guidance code' for the movie came up on the screen. It said something like 'violence, adult themes, sex scenes, nudity, coarse language . . . '. Sam read the information from the screen aloud and then said: 'Wow, this'll be good. Can I watch it?' I quizzed her a little about her choice of what was a 'good' movie and she said, in summary, that she always read the information in the TV guide and on the screen to work out what movies she wanted to watch and the more warnings there were the better the movie would be: 'Like, if it's just adult themes, that's probably pretty boring, but if it's adult themes, nudity and coarse language then it's probably a good movie.'

I regard the story above as an example of what I will call *subversive critical literacy*. Sam had taken information intended for adults to use to help them decide what their children should watch and turned it around completely by using it as a guide to what she thought she'd like to watch. The point that arises from this is that once critical literacy and critical thinking skills are developed (or developing) in children they don't always proceed along the lines that their carers have mapped out for them. If you teach children to think for themselves, it's quite likely that that's exactly what they will do.

The next part of this chapter concentrates on using a small amount of linguistic terminology and analysis to help to develop critical literacy. To do this I have chosen three pop songs. What I intend to do is to analyse how gender is constructed in these songs: how women (and men) are positioned. The songs are: *My Boyfriend's Back*, *You Don't Own Me* and *I Am Woman*. I am using these songs as examples only but with the intention of showing how critical literacy might be integrated with specific language work. The songs span close enough to two decades, from the late 1950s and early 1960s to the late 1970s.

As a first step I will be doing a small amount of linguistic analysis on the songs. In my analysis I have taken a few liberties with the finer points of linguistic analysis. I've kept it fairly straightforward because my purpose is to present something that might be possible to use in the classroom as part of the students' language work. The language analysis is intended both as a prelude to and to run concurrent with a critical appraisal of the songs as manifestations of broader social issues.

In analysing the language of the songs I will focus on several variables and how they interact with each other. In the main I will focus on the participant roles that women (and men) are given in the songs: for example, whether they are the actors or the acted on: whether they are the 'doers' or the 'done to'. I will do this using as little technical linguistic terminology as I can but still demonstrate that even a little bit can enhance a critical reading of text.

Analysis

The songs are analysed by looking at the participants (the 'doers' and the 'done to'), what kinds of processes (verbs) the participants are engaging in and whether what is going on is either positive or negative (ie if the verb has a 'not' in front of it or if there is some kind of negative effect). Participants, verbs, and positives and negatives are then matched up to see what the woman's role in the song is. I will attempt to present the analyses as classroom exercises.

> **KEY TO ANALYSIS**
> Participants doing the 'doing' (actors) are shown in **bold**. Participants being acted on or 'done to' are shown in ***bold italics***.
>
> Verbs (and auxiliary verbs) underlined.

Also, as purists will notice, I have taken a few liberties with the technical details of the analysis. I have ignored elements such as embedded clauses and have used the term *actor* for all participants who are the 'doers', 'be-ers' and 'sayers'.

The purpose of doing this as a class exercise is to provide an initial focus on the specifics of the language of the songs in order to build skills in language analysis which, hopefully, can be transferred to other contexts.

Finding 'doing' and 'being' words

As a first step we need to work out what kind of action is going on in the songs: kind of who's doing what to whom. At this stage we are concentrating on identifying who is involved in the action and whether they are the 'doer' or the 'done to'. This could also be done as a classroom exercise with the students using some code to identify the participants.

MY BOYFRIEND'S BACK (Feldman-Gottehrer)

(spoken)
He <u>went</u> away, and **you** <u>hung</u> around
And <u>bothered</u> ***me***, every night
And when **I** <u>wouldn't go out</u> with you,
You <u>said</u> things that <u>weren't</u> very nice.

(sung)
My boyfriend<u>'s</u> back, and there<u>'s gonna be</u> trouble (Hey la, hey la, **my** boyfriend<u>'s</u> back)
When **you** <u>see</u> **him** <u>comin'</u>, better <u>cut out</u> on the double (Hey la, hey la, my **boyfriend**<u>'s</u> back)
He<u>'s</u> <u>been</u> straight in life, while **I** <u>was</u> untrue (Hey la, hey la, **my boyfriend**<u>'s</u> back)
So look out now, cause **he**<u>'s</u> <u>comin'</u> after ***you*** (Hey la, hey la, **my boyfriend**<u>'s</u> back)

(Hey, **he** <u>knows</u> that **you**<u>'ve been tryin'</u>)
(And **he** <u>knows</u> that **you**<u>'ve been lyin'</u>)

He<u>'s</u> <u>been</u> gone for such a long time
(Hey la, hey la, **my boyfriend**<u>'s</u> back)
Now **he**<u>'s</u> back and things <u>are</u> real fine
(Hey la, hey la, **my boyfriend**<u>'s</u> back)
You<u>'re gonna be</u> sorry **you** were ever <u>born</u> (Hey la, hey la, **my boyfriend**<u>'s</u> back)
Cause **he**<u>'s</u> kinda big and **he**<u>'s</u> awful strong (Hey la, hey la, **my boyfriend**<u>'s</u> back)

(Hey, **he** <u>knows</u> **I** <u>wasn't cheatin'</u>)
(Now, ***you***<u>'re gonna get</u> a beatin')

What made **you** <u>think</u> **he**'d <u>believe</u> all your lies, wahoo . . . wahoo . . . **You**<u>'re</u> a big man now but **he**<u>'ll</u> <u>cut</u> ***you*** down to size, wahoo . . . wahoo . . . <u>Wait</u> and <u>see</u>!

My boyfriend<u>'s</u> back, **he**<u>'s gonna save *my* reputation</u> (Hey la, hey la, **my boyfriend**<u>'s</u> back)
If **I** <u>were</u> **you** I'd <u>take</u> a permanent vacation (Hey la, hey la, **my boyfriend**<u>'s</u> back)
Yeah, **my boyfriend**<u>'s</u> back . . .

©EMI Blackwood Music Inc

YOU DON'T OWN ME (Madara-White)

You don't own me
I'm not just one of your many toys
You don't own me
Don't say I can't go with other boys

Don't tell me what to do
Don't tell me what to say
An' please, when I go out with you
Don't put me on display

You don't own me
Don't try to change me in anyway
You don't own me
Don't tie me down 'cause I'll never stay

I don't tell you what to say
I don't tell you what to do
So just let me be myself
That's all I ask of you

I'm young and I love to be young
I'm free and I love to be free
To live my life the way I want
To say and do whatever I please

©Merjoda Music Inc/Unichappell Music Inc

I AM WOMAN (Reddy-Burton)

I am woman, hear me roar
In numbers too big to ignore
And I know too much to go back an' pretend
'cause I've heard it all before
And I've been down there on the floor
No one's ever gonna keep me down again

(chorus)
Oh yes I am wise
But it's wisdom born of pain
Yes, I've paid the price
But look how much I gained
If I have to, I can do anything
I am strong (strong)
I am invincible (invincible)
I am woman

You <u>can</u> <u>bend</u> but <u>never break</u> **me**
'cause it only <u>serves to make</u> me
More determined <u>to achieve</u> ***my final goal***
And **I** <u>come back</u> even stronger
Not a novice any longer
'cause **you**'<u>ve</u> <u>deepened</u> ***the conviction in my soul***

(chorus)
I <u>am</u> woman <u>watch</u> **me** <u>grow</u>
<u>See</u> **me** <u>standing</u> toe to toe
As **I** <u>spread</u> ***my lovin' arms*** across the land
But **I**'<u>m</u> still an embryo
With a long long way to go
Until **I** <u>make</u> ***my brother*** <u>understand</u>

Oh yes **I** <u>am</u> wise
But it'<u>s</u> wisdom born of pain
Yes, **I**'<u>ve</u> <u>paid</u> the price
But <u>look</u> how much **I** <u>gained</u>
If **I** <u>have to</u> **I** <u>can face</u> anything
I <u>am</u> strong (strong)
I <u>am</u> invincible (invincible)
I <u>am</u> woman
Oh, **I** <u>am</u> woman
I <u>am</u> invincible
I <u>am</u> strong

(fade)
I <u>am</u> woman
I <u>am</u> invincible
I <u>am</u> strong
I <u>am</u> woman

©Irving Music Inc/Buggerlugs Music Inc

Building on the language work

Just working out who's doing what to whom is a step towards a critical reading of the texts. For example, in *My Boyfriend's Back*, although the song is sung by a female all the action is done, or is going to be done, by men. The female's role in the song is the prize that men fight over. *You Don't Own Me* is also sung by a female singer. In this song the female participant has much more of an active role in the song, asserting what she wants and does not want in resistance to male domination. In *I am Woman* the female (a generic female rather than an individual one: all women rather than one woman) plays the leading role in her own right. The song comes across as an anthem.

The next step is to add in a couple more variables and see what kind of picture we can draw up. One possibility is to look at the polarity of the processes the participants are engaged in. By this I mean whether they are *is* or *is not*: positive or negative. We could add to this what kind of process (verb) the participants are engaged in. I will classify the verbs according to whether they are verbs of 'doing', 'thinking/feeling', 'saying' or 'being'. Add to this schema the gender of the participant and it is possible to draw up a table like the one below. The table is for *You Don't Own Me*.

Stanza	Participant	M or F	actor Y or N	positive or negative	verb type
1	you	M	Y	neg	having
	me	F	N		
	I	F	Y	neg	being
	you	M	Y		having
	me	F	N	neg	
	(you)	M	Y		saying
	I	F	Y	neg	doing
2	(you)	M	Y	neg	having
	me	F	N		
	(you)	M	Y	neg	doing
	me	F	N		
	I	F	Y	pos	doing
	you	M	N		
	(you)	M	Y	neg	doing
	me	F	N		
3	you	M	Y	neg	having
	me	F	N		
	(you)	M	Y	neg	doing
	me	F	N		
	you	M	Y	neg	having
	me	F	N		
	(you)	M	Y	neg	doing
	me	F	N		
	I	F	Y	neg	doing

Stanza	Participant	M or F	actor Y or N	positive or negative	verb type
4	I	F	Y	neg	saying/saying
	you	M	N		
	I	F	Y	neg	saying/doing
	you	M	N		
	(you)	M	Y	pos	doing/being
	me	F	N		
	I	F	Y	pos	being/saying
	you	M	N		
5	I	F	Y	pos	being
	I	F	Y	pos	feeling
	I	F	Y	pos	being
	I	F	Y	pos	feeling
	I	F	Y	pos	doing/feeling
	I	F	Y	pos	saying/doing

We now have a table that shows us who is doing what to whom, what kind of action is going on and whether the action is being treated as positive or negative. Some potentially interesting patterns emerge from this table. If we look at the combination of female participant and polarity we find the following pattern.

For the first three stanzas of the song we find a woman who is resisting being constructed as a possession. Her participant role is constructed principally as that of 'done to' or 'acted upon' and her resistance is encoded in the negative polarity (ie *don't* own, *don't* try, *don't* tell). From the perspective of her participant role she is, for the most part, resisting actions that she feels that a man is trying to impose upon her. For example in the verbs *don't own, don't tell, don't put, don't try to change*, she is resisting material and verbal action initiated by a male. When she is the actor, it is what she is not rather than what she is that she asserts (eg *I'm not just one of your many toys, 'cause I'll never stay*).

Things start to change in the fourth and fifth stanzas. The fourth stanza comes across as a demand for equality, or at least for reciprocity; but still, in the first two lines it is in the negative (*I don't tell you*) although with the female as actor. The final two lines of the stanza switch to positive polarity: a plea for autonomy. The autonomy, however, still has to be asked for.

The final stanza represents a major shift in the song. For the first time the female participant asserts herself as herself in positive terms with herself as the actor. Interestingly enough, in this stanza the male disappears as a participant.

The same kind of table could be drawn up for the other two songs. I won't do it here, but to summarise, we would find marked differences in how the songs construct the the role of women and the kinds of assumptions they embody about being female.

In *My Boyfriend's Back* we find a female who constructs herself as being almost incidental in the lives of males. The song is sung by a woman but she takes little part in the action. She appears as the actor three times: *I wouldn't go out with you*; *I was untrue* (it is not explained how she was untrue); and *I wasn't cheatin'* (an apparent contradiction with the previous example). In each case her 'doing' or 'being' is framed negatively: what she didn't do or what she wasn't.

She does, however, endorse male action on her behalf. The trouble brewing in the song is trouble that is going to be resolved between males. *My boyfriend* is constructed in the role of protector and saviour: he's *going to cut you down to size* and *save my reputation*. The other male is the 'baddie' who *bothered*, *hung around* and *said things that weren't very nice*. Presumably the boyfriend has to actually fulfil his obligations as saviour before he wins the prize. In fact, it should be noted that the male roles in this song are just as much socially constructed as the female role. If he is to maintain his role as protector and saviour, the boyfriend has few choices: he is more or less obliged to give the unwanted male a *beatin'* and make him sorry he was ever born. Luckily for him *he's kinda big and he's awful strong* so presumably he has the physical attributes to play his part.

Critical literacy activities

I suggest that analysis of a song such as this opens up room for much critical discussion about questions of gender roles. For example, here are a few possible points that could be raised in discussion:

- Is it necessary for females to have to rely on males to save them?
- As a first option, why couldn't the female participant just tell the other guy to leave her alone?
- Does, or should, a female's *reputation* depend on males?
- What kind of stress would the boyfriend be under if he was 'kinda skinny and not real strong'?

In *I am Woman* we find the opposite. Men are almost incidental to the text although I read the text as a combination of an anthem of at least partial triumph by women over domination by men and a rallying cry to marshal forces to continue the struggle. Interestingly enough, men are not mentioned in the song but are addressed either indirectly or in the second person. For instance, the 'no-one' in *no-one's ever gonna keep me down again* is presumably male. Likewise, the 'you' in *you can bend but never break me* presumably represents generic man.

There are only two participants in *I am Woman*, a generic female *I* (representing all females) and a generic male, *You/No-one/my brother* (representing all males. Of these the female participant is the principal actor. She is the one who *is*, who *knows*, who's *paid*, *gained* and so on. The polarity is also always positive when positive qualities are involved (*I am strong, I am invincible, I can do anything*). All of the positive qualities of woman outweigh the work of man, who has tried to keep *woman down there on the floor*, caused her *pain*, extracted a *price*. All this has 'bent' but not 'broken' her and only served to make her stronger.

I am Woman, however, is not unproblematic. It uses the analogy of warfare to construct male–female relations and it constructs female strength as something which arises from the struggle against men rather than something that exists in its own right. In this sense, even the image of the strong, assertive, independent female is constructed in relation to males: as a worthy, even superior, opponent.

A couple of potential discussion questions I would raise about this song are: do female–male relations have to be constructed as warfare or might there be more productive analogies? (Note that I am saying this as a male.)

If we look at the songs collectively there is a pattern change in the female roles. First, in *My Boyfriend's Back*, we find a female who recognises and is both compliant with and endorses male authority. In *You Don't Own Me*, we find a female resisting male domination and asserting her own right to equality and reciprocity. While in *I am Woman*, we find both a shift from the woman as an individual to women collectively as a participant and a female role portrayed as a potential victor. In looking at the three songs, I see *You Don't Own Me* as an intermediate, or transitional step and, perhaps because of this I find it the most interesting.

Rounding off

If we extrapolate from the individual songs, what can we say? How can a critical appraisal of songs such as these contribute to how young people, male and female, see how they are positioned in the world by language such as song lyrics (and the social practices in which they are embedded)? First, everyone is born into a world where gender plays an important part in the construction of social relations, and upper primary school children are at a point in their lives when their awareness of gender relations is emerging. Thus, it seems to me to be very important for these students to develop some critical awareness of 'gender'—and the kinds of positionings that result from different social assumptions about gender—are always social constructions and are not simply unchallengeable 'givens'.

Before closing, a word of advice. Teachers who are keen to work with a systemic functional linguistic approach to critical literacy, but who are a little nervous about using this grammatical system, may want to focus—at least for starters—on just *one* aspect of the linguistic analysis (say, for example, identifying 'actors' in a song's lyrics or other text). Once confidence in and fluency with that particular aspect of linguistic analysis (and the kind of work it can be made to do in a critical literacy approach) is developed, then another aspect can be tackled, and so on.

Knowledge about how language works gives students an explicit and tangible point of reference from which to both generalise from and to offer as evidence for what they say in response their analyses. Following this line of reasoning, I suggest that integrating some explicit language work with the critical analysis of texts in the context of a social concept such as 'gender' gives students an explicit set of effective analytical tools to work with and will enable them to examine and evaluate relationships between language choices and the construction of social roles in everyday life.

CHAPTER 5

Theory and spice, and things not nice: Popular culture in the primary classroom

RAY MISSON

Ray Misson describes the careful balancing act required between pleasure and critique when investigating popular texts in the primary classroom. He affirms the importance of deconstructing and critically analysing such texts, while drawing attention to the need to recognise that popular texts are attractive and pleasurable. Using such diverse examples as *Titanic*, the Spice Girls and the *Goosebumps* book series, Misson illustrates how to extend students' pleasure and enjoyment of popular texts through an analysis of the ways in which the texts work.

One of the major features of popular texts, whether we are looking at *Titanic* or *Friends*, *Dolly* magazine or The Wiggles, is that they are easily and readily accessible, whereas one of the major features of academic work on popular culture is its high level of theoretical sophistication. This should not surprise us. Popular texts usually present themselves as straightforward and approachable, with their ways of working and the beliefs they are promoting highly naturalised (ie made to appear natural and not the result of construction). However, complex conceptual frameworks and strategies are often necessary, to overcome the surface resistance of this appearance of openness and to make the texts available for detailed analysis.

This makes work on popular texts—and therefore popular culture—in primary schools rather problematic. There is no doubt that popular texts should be looked at because they are such powerful shapers of the students' perceptions of the world, but to do serious work on them seems to require a level of intellectual understanding beyond what could reasonably be expected of (or, some might say, developed in) the primary school child.

And, it could be asked, is such 'serious work' inappropriate for younger children anyway, who might be better left alone to enjoy popular texts without nagging adult worries about the ideological beliefs being promoted or their exploitiveness? Mightn't such analysis kill the innocent enjoyment of childhood, the ability of the young to become involved in fictional worlds and to commit themselves to the excitement of what they have to offer?

It is to this question that we will turn first, before looking at what it is in popular texts that might be examined in class, and how teachers might best go about developing the ability to critique the texts in the primary school child.

Popular texts and pleasure

The case for looking at popular texts is very easy to make. Popular texts are ubiquitous and, without question, very powerful. We live in a world shaped by the mass media and by the mass manufacture of products available for our consumption, commodities—or things or services—that we desire to possess and through which we come to see ourselves as particular kinds of people. Most children spend a great deal of time watching television. They are also a major target market, most obviously for toy and game manufacturers. One does not want to be superior about this. The child who desperately wants a Barbie campervan or a Sony PlayStation or a Tamagotchi for his or her birthday is essentially no different from the adult who wants an electronic organiser or the *Boogie Nights* soundtrack or a copper-base frying pan. In all these cases, the thing is wanted not only for the use that can be got out of it, but because the person sees themselves as the kind of person who owns a Barbie campervan, a copper-base frying pan, or whatever. In other words, the objects we desire are a statement to the world, and even more potently to ourselves, about how we see ourselves and how we want to be seen.

Similarly, the texts we read or watch in our leisure time are a powerful indicator of our self-perception, particularly those we declare to be our favourites. These favourite texts must be especially congruent with our desires, and reflect back to us both a version of the world that at some deep level we find satisfying or exciting, and a pleasing image of how it might be if we lived as an idealised self within that world. This is no less true if our involvement with the text is the result of advertising, publicity or other media hype. The hype has given the text a particular value as something desirable to possess or use, and we are subscribing to that value by consuming the text. We become the kind of person—identify with millions of other people—who would never miss *Seinfeld* or *ER* or (to use an extended notion of 'text') who would want every new accessory for our Barbie doll.

All this makes it particularly difficult to handle popular texts effectively in the classroom if one wants to do anything more than chat about them. In particular, it suggests a light and sensitive touch is needed (when you treat my favourite program, tread softly, because you tread on my dreams). If our students' personalities and self-perceptions are bound up with these texts, then it is not likely to be productive to come in with a battery of techniques to rip these popular texts apart and show them to be sorry, worthless things.

Thus, it seems to me that the first principle in working with any popular text is to acknowledge and understand its attractiveness. If you simply cannot understand why anyone would ever become interested in or excited by the text, then you probably ought not to be handling it. You are likely to be simply negative and destructive and therefore set yourself *against* your students rather than work *with* them.

All popular texts work by inviting involvement, by offering pleasure. To return to our earlier question, why would we want, particularly with children, to spoil their pleasure? I suppose there are two (contradictory) answers to that question. The first is, we wouldn't. The second is, because it's bad for them. The first answer comes from a recognition that pleasure is important in itself, and that when that pleasure is felt as a significant expression of the personality, then destroying it is potentially a limitation of the range of being available to the person. The second answer recognises that, precisely because the pleasure is what establishes certain beliefs in the child, these beliefs may be unacceptable or harmful (sexist beliefs, racist beliefs, beliefs that violence is the best solution to problems) and must be countered if we want to develop what we see as more positive attitudes.

So, in dealing with popular texts, teachers often walk a tightrope, not wishing to set themselves against students' judgments, but at the same time wanting students to see the possibly damaging limitations of the texts they are consuming. If a teacher points out the limitations of *Home and Away*, she or he can be cast as staidly negative; if the text is allowed simply to do its ideological work unnoticed, then the teacher is scarcely taking on the responsibilities of an effective critical literacy teacher in making students aware of what the text is asking them to believe.

Thankfully, however, the tightrope actually doesn't seem to be particularly difficult to negotiate, as long as one maintains the sense of pleasure in the text and doesn't allow the critique to dominate completely. If someone is enjoying a text, further pleasure can usually be taken in looking at how it is working on the reader or viewer. The sheer cleverness with which it operates can be noted and appreciated, while at the same time, through making clear the source of its effect, its messages can be, to some extent at least, made available for critical analysis. It is only if a teacher assumes that the purpose of analysis is to destroy the pleasure so as to destroy the possibility of the text imposing its beliefs on readers or viewers that she or he goes seriously astray. If the pleasure is allowed, a great deal of very valuable work can be done.

We can now turn to look at some ways of working on and with popular texts.

Approaching popular texts

The basic principle underlying work on popular texts in a critical literacy framework, as on any texts, is that we need to show their 'constructedness', to show that they are not an innocent representation of reality but have been created for a particular purpose. There are two (related) major kinds of purpose that a teacher might be concerned to make explicit, and they produce different—although complementary—understandings of popular texts, which we will examine in the rest of this chapter. The first is concerned with the way the texts are constructed to appeal to a certain target audience (or group of consumers), and so we might see the constructedness as arising from a commercial purpose. The second is concerned with the conscious or unconscious transmission of particular values, and so can be related to an ideological purpose.

In fact, these two perspectives—the commercial and the ideological—are the basis of one of the recurrent issues in popular culture: whether the texts reflect popular opinion or whether they are shaping it. When the ideological work being done by girls' magazines or by cartoons or by other popular phenomena is decried, the producers either deny that their texts have such an impact, or, more often, defend themselves with some such idea that they are 'just giving the public what they want'. In other words, they have done their market research and they are reflecting the audience's fantasies, providing what gives them pleasure. Others, of course, argue that the whole process is nowhere near so innocent as this suggests; rather, that the big corporations that produce these texts have a vested interest in maintaining a conservative view of the world, and so will produce nothing that cannot finally be reconciled with, and assimilated into, mainstream beliefs, and so confirm and maintain the dominant ideology.

We do not need to linger long over this argument. Quite clearly the texts are produced to sell, and so are created with the purpose of pleasing a particular 'target' audience. Equally clearly, this has a deeply ideological outcome. If the texts reflect the audience's fantasies, provide a mirror of how they want to see themselves—how they feel themselves to be deep down when all the superficial inadequacies are stripped away—then quite clearly they are doing highly significant ideological work (see Althusser, 1970, for a highly influential theorisation of this view). This is why the commercial perspective and the ideological perspective are so closely connected, although we can treat them separately as different elements of the same process.

Commercial questions

If you are working with a particular popular cultural phenomenon, then the easiest way into analysis is often to ask to what particular audience the text seems to be targeted. This is not an aggressive question: any student would acknowledge with any text that it is created with an audience in mind, even though it might be a very broad audience. Even with a text with the very broadest appeal, such as James Cameron's *Titanic,* it is easy to start discussion on how it has been constructed to give that broad appeal, and to consider which different parts of the film are geared to pleasing different sectors in the audience, even if only at the level of talking about the 'bits for the chicks' and the 'bits for the guys'.

The next question can often be, how do we know that this is the target audience? The answer is usually couched in terms of the content being 'the kind of thing that that sort of person likes'. The girls like the romance, the boys like the special effects. We are perhaps entering dangerous territory here, territory rife with essentialism, stereotyping, binaries and many other things that set off warning bells in well-read critical literacy teachers. Indeed, you can ask the question about whether it is true that girls are most interested in the romance, boys in the special effects, and hopefully at least get enough variety in the responses to undercut simple assumptions and associations. However, it is perhaps better at this stage simply to press further in trying to identify the kinds of interests being assumed, because this profiles the kind of person that the text is assuming the reader to be or become. It also draws attention to the ways in which the text is being constructed to please a target reader or viewer, rather than simply to reflect the world. Let us take a more detailed example.

One of the major entertainment phenomena of the last third of the twentieth century has been 'the group'. This undoubtedly started with the Beatles. There were, of course, groups before the Beatles, but the Beatles changed our conception of what a pop group 'is'. Indeed, the Beatles themselves played out the transformation. I claim no authority as a pop historian, and I cannot remember pop music before the Beatles all that clearly, but if one thinks of what one knows of earlier groups (the Andrews Sisters, the Everley Brothers, Bill Haley and the Comets), the emphasis is on homogeneity. There are simple harmonies: the bands tend to be shown wearing identical clothes on stage. This is true of the early Beatles, but, of course, over their comparatively short career, they developed musically into a much more complex, multi-layered sound, and as performers into a much more complex unit that played on difference rather than similarity (it would be interesting to go back to the newspapers of the time to see if earlier groups were said to 'split up', or whether some other term such as 'stop performing together' or 'retire' was used. The common current myth of the life of pop groups—garage to stardom to splitting up and pursuing solo careers—is based on the Beatles, and is premised on the members of the group increasingly asserting their individuality).

Everyone had a favourite Beatle, just as these days, their children or grandchildren have a favourite Spice Girl or Wiggle. The Spice Girls and The Wiggles provide a fruitful source for analysis in these terms, partly because they are very much media-constructed groups, and there isn't even a pretence that they are a natural flowering of the suburban garage. Quite clearly choices have been made (whether by managers, record companies or the group members themselves doesn't matter) to bring together and project particular kinds of personalities.

Given this assumption, and it is probably an assumption that even the most ardent Spice Girls or Wiggles fan would not feel to be too threatening, we can ask why this particular combination of people has been found to be so appealing and so popular. One of the answers is obviously to do with the range of personalities covered, as is particularly evident with the Spice Girls. Most girls can find a fantasy ideal to project themselves into within the group, or (less significantly) boys can find a possible image to match their fantasies. This is made almost ludicrously obvious in the case of the Spice Girls, in that their names have all the blatant directness of a medieval allegory: Ginger Spice, Baby Spice, Posh Spice, Sporty Spice and Scary Spice. We are very obviously directed to the kind of person each one is, and so to the qualities we might admire and/or identify with in them. The group is developed to be adored as a whole, but, even more, it is a group with which we are expected and encouraged to have a favourite.

It would be a very simple strategy when working with kids, to ask them to describe what they understand about the character of each, and to speculate on why they were chosen. Even better would be to have them imagine another group of Spice Girls with different names and different personalities: Pony Spice, Swinging Spice, Teacher Spice, Outer Spice—the possibilities are indeed endless! They could then consider whether they thought the group they have conceived would be as popular. Then, of course, the tragic exit of Ginger Spice in recent times might not be all bad news in that it does allow for a variant of this work. The students can be asked to imagine a replacement for Ginger (or any other group member who might subsequently leave). This would almost certainly bring home the need for careful balancing of personalities in the group in order to maximise audience appeal across as broad a spectrum as possible. One could, of course, set up the task so as to produce parody, but in many ways it is more interesting if the group is imagined as a genuine alternative, since this undercuts the uniqueness of the original group and affirms its constructedness even more.

This business of having favourites, incidentally, has become a dominant feature of popular culture. You only have to think of the difference between the sitcoms we were watching a few years ago, and the most popular ones currently showing. Whereas it was certainly possible to be particularly attracted to certain people in earlier family sitcoms (Michael J Fox in *Family Ties*, Kirk Cameron—or, in the last series, Leonardo di Caprio—in *Growing Pains*,) and whereas there were certainly ensemble sitcoms such as *Cheers* in the past, there was nothing like the equality of attractiveness and significance across the ensemble as we have in shows such as *Seinfeld* or *Friends*, or indeed in drama series such as *ER* or *Chicago Hope*, although they have an obvious predecessor in serial soaps (on this aspect of *Seinfeld*, see Misson 1995).

A popular phenomenon such as the Spice Girls is in some ways an easy subject to work on, because there is so much readily available media material that can be used. The passionate interest generated by the group also makes it easy: students would rather talk about the Spice Girls than not. They are such a ready topic of conversation outside the classroom because of media saturation, that it is easy to bring the discussion into the classroom, activate a range of views, and frame the material in quite interesting ways. There are other phenomena with which such transformation is less easy, and we now turn to one of these to look at ways in which beliefs inherent in these phenomena might be made available for discussion. As we will see, the whole venture becomes more difficult and perhaps questionable as the material becomes more intractable.

Identifying ideology

Horror and the supernatural have become big business. For a wide general audience, we only have to point to the success of *The X-Files* to establish this; for a younger audience, we only have to mention the word *Goosebumps*. The works of Stephen King are still massively popular, although perhaps a bit less so than a few years past, and more commonly (but certainly not exclusively) with older readers than primary school children. Other writers such as Christopher Pike still command big audiences. The *Goosebumps* books have been joined by an array of other horror/supernatural series, including book versions of *The X-Files*, that fill the children's bookshelves in newsagents, almost pushing such things as the horsy books and the Newspaper Kids off altogether.

The adult reader venturing into this material is unlikely to be impressed by the literary qualities of what she or he will meet. The adult reader indeed is going to find it hard to experience and acknowledge the attractiveness of the material at all, at the same time perhaps as seeing all too clearly what that attractiveness is. This is especially true of the books that target a younger audience, such as in series like *Goosebumps*, *Creepers* or *Hair-Raisers*.

Again, I claim no deep expertise. I have read a number of titles recently, but given the range available, it is possible that they are not representative (although I doubt it—the books give the impression of operating on a tried-and-true formula). Coming from a background of reading Stephen King and watching the odd episode of *The X-Files*, the immediately striking things about this material include:

- the lack of serious victims: the young protagonists are lone crusaders against the supernatural evil, but the 'horror' tends not to be established through harm to lesser characters that registers as mattering;
- a concentration on sheer grossness: there is a high 'yuck-factor' in all of the books;

- a tone that is always ready to modulate into humour to deflate any moment when the horror is likely to become genuinely scary: it is a tone that maintains a relentless normality.

As I say, you can easily see the attractions, even if you don't feel them yourself. They are the attractions of being transgressive, and of participating in the adventures of the hero (or less often, the heroine) defending the natural against the supernatural, the normal against the abnormal. The transgression isn't against the normal limitations of day-to-day existence—the 'natural'—but against the demands of ordinary decorum. It is basically a variation on toilet humour, a reveling in the messiness of bodily functions and fluids:

> (Our heroes, in *Loco-Zombies*, have got themselves inside the belly of the Zombie Master, who is in the shape of a giant maggot.)
>
> We rush along the slime-infested tunnel of maggot flesh, trying desperately not to touch anything. Zombie heads, arms and legs lurch out at us, snapping and groping. We jump and dodge as dead fingers claw at our eyes. I feel as if I am being poisoned by the putrid smell and the dripping mucus that splatters me,
> 'This is a bummer!' says Boris . . .
> Behind us I hear a gurgling and gushing.
> 'What's that?'
> 'I hope it isn't what I think it is!' says Nat.
> The sound is like a thousand toilets flushing but more slurpy, as though the water's not water but huge chunks of maggot mud. It's right behind us, heading towards us like an express train with no brakes and a zombie at the wheel!
> 'Go!' screams Nat, '*Hurry!*'
> But it's flashing towards us—too fast for us to escape!
> We're about to surf the most horrible wave in the universe!
>
> (Condon and Hood 1996, pp 46–47)

The passage makes the point about toilet humour particularly well, but it is not at all atypical either in the subject matter or the tone. These children remain remarkably blasé and ready to crack a joke in the face of quite extraordinary adversity (and worse). There is a kind of exhilaration, a revelling in the foulness and messiness of it all.

It is hard to know how such material might be used safely in the classroom. Indeed, the material often sets itself resolutely against school. In one R L Stine book, the teacher is one of the walking dead come from her grave to choose a victim, and only our hero recognises that there is something strange about her (Stine 1995). Even in a time of pending teacher shortages, the recruitment procedures for this school obviously require investigation. (Incidentally, unobtrusively on the publishing details page, there is the line 'Written by Stephen Roos'. Is nothing authentic in this world?) In such cases as this, many a teacher might think it best to leave well enough alone. The kids enjoy the books; part of that enjoyment is that they transgress decorum and adult institutions; why intervene in a way that invades the students' private pleasures and might spoil the fun? The only reason would be because the texts are so popular, and the literacy classroom ought to be open to all kinds of texts.

The most obvious (although not necessarily the most productive) way into the books may be through looking at their representations of race and/or gender. There is sometimes a tendency either to identify the supernatural Other with the racial Other—there are after all popular traditions of the mystical East and of the necromantic Middle European—or indeed to substitute another kind of Otherness for the supernatural. In one book, an Asian 'businessman' abducts a pair of twins and has strange body organ removals and transplants performed on them (Clark 1996). The reactions to the supernatural are also usually gendered, although care is taken to avoid the obvious stereotypes and consequent charges of sexism. The female tends to be the down-to-earth practical type rather than the terrified or squeamish type. In other words, the girls play the mother figure rather than the helpless heroine. It is noteworthy that the wise-cracking smart-aleck reactions that are a common feature are always associated with the males (at least in the examples of the genre I have read). This might provide fruitful grounds for analysis of current versions of gender in popular texts.

The analysis of race or gender representations, however, is limited. Students very quickly get used to providing teachers with the answers they want when it comes to looking at gender or ethnic construction, and such routines probably don't effect very deep shifts in understanding about social disadvantage. Perhaps a better way into working with this material would be through treating it as a case study in genre. If students had read a range of the books, it would be easy to profile the generic features, looking at the kinds of people who are the heroes, the nature of the supernatural element, and the characteristic story lines. One would need to be open to acknowledging a range. The books giving novelisations of episodes from *The X-Files* are obviously rather different from books like *Loco-Zombies* or the *Goosebumps* series. Indeed, a useful strategy would be to contrast *Goosebumps* with *The X-Files* or with Stephen King or Christopher Pike books if there were any King or Pike fans in the class.

Having established the major generic features, the question of why the genre might have developed in this particular way could be examined. This would be done best in terms of how the generic features engage the reader. After all, for any popular genre to evolve and become popular, it must be congruent with some deep fantasies within the social psyche. To question what the features of the genre call on in their readers is to recognise that the texts are structured to produce particular effects within a particular social context.

What is it that people find interesting and exciting about the supernatural? Why is there the emphasis on physical grossness, and why do we (some of us anyway) find this exhilarating? In particular, we might ask what are the qualities that we are meant to admire in the heroes in the face of the slimy decomposing horrors they are forced to confront? The supernatural tale is usually a tale of good versus evil. It is about a threat to normal society that must be overcome. The qualities that permit the protagonists to conquer the horrible outside force and come through unscathed are clearly the ones that we are meant to admire.

How critical we would want to be of any of this is open to question. The books seem fairly harmless. They are generally careful to be (superficially) inclusive, which is comparatively simple when you set up such an obvious Other outside the realms of the natural. We certainly don't want to treat zombies or vampires as unfortunate outsiders who ought to be woven into the social fabric. In some ways, the aspect of the books one most wants to criticise is their tendency to underplay the terror, and the way they usually substitute an easy smartness for what one might consider an appropriate reaction. This goes hand in hand with a feature common in children's popular texts: the isolation of the child from an uncomprehending adult world that leaves the child to deal with dangers alone. One can see the fantasy being played on, but it's one that any adult would try to question at her or his own risk. Anyway, it is probably a big enough step towards critical literacy to make explicit the basic attractions of the genre and the way the texts work to involve us, showing that they are constructed to make us see the world in certain ways. More stringent critique is an advance that can wait.

Working with popular texts always creates exciting classes, as long as the teacher is willing to allow the students time and space to air their enthusiasm and their expertise, and is able to harness that enthusiasm and expertise rather than trying to stand out against it. It ought never to be a matter of setting the enjoyment of the texts against a critical understanding. Rather, there should always be an acknowledgment and a demonstration that the enjoyment and critique can coexist very comfortably and productively.

References

Althusser, L (1984, 1970) 'Ideology and ideological state apparatuses: Notes towards an Investigation', *Essays on Ideology*. London: Verso.
Clark, M (1996) *Body Parts*. Sydney: Mark Macleod.
Condon, B and Hood R (1996) *Loco-Zombies*. Sydney: Hodder.
Misson, R (1995) 'Living the lifestyle: The attractions of *Seinfeld*', *Australian Journal of Comedy*. Vol 1, No 2, pp 55–75.
Steinberg, S and Kincheloe, J (1997) (eds) *Kinderculture: The Corporate Construction of Childhood*. Boulder, Colorado: Westview Press.
Stine, R L (1995) *Ghosts of Fear Street*. New York: Minstrel.

CHAPTER 6

'When you only have girls as friends, you got some serious problems': Interrogating masculinities in the literacy classroom

WAYNE MARTINO

The activities described in this chapter are based on the use of reader-response strategies that involve self-reflection and self-evaluation. Wayne Martino demonstrates that students already know how to use these strategies and that this knowledge can be used to analyse students' possible 'ways of being in the world'. Specifically, Martino focuses on a group of adolescent boys and their responses to a set of written profiles. He argues that these responses can be used by teachers to assist students to critically evaluate the forms of masculinity available to them.

Analysing 'gender' is a recurring process in critical literacy activities in classrooms. I have become increasingly aware of the need to analyse—and have students engage with—the ways in which young adolescent males have been enculturated into certain ways of 'being male' and how this affects the ways in which they perceive and judge this in others.

In most societies like our own, a particular form (or version) of masculinity will always be dominant and used by many people to police the boundaries of what is considered to be appropriate behaviour for boys and men. Recent research highlights the kinds of problems boys have in learning how to relate to one another as particular kinds of males (see, for example, Butler, 1996; Connell 1989, 1995; Epstein 1997; Jordan 1995; Kehily and Nayak 1997; Mac an Ghaill 1994; Martino 1997; Nyack and Kehily 1996; Parker 1996; Walker 1988).

Problems are generated by, or include:

- having to prove that they are tough
- denigrating anything that smacks of femininity or homosexuality

- engaging in forms of sex-based harassment directed at both girls and those boys who don't 'measure up' to macho norms
- engaging in risk-taking practices which may be detrimental to their health and well-being
- using 'put downs' and 'giving crap to' or teasing others to act 'cool'
- endorsing forms of homophobia and violence as means of asserting their heterosexuality.

The literacy classroom is a productive site for undertaking a critical kind of practice that helps students develop capacities and strategies for analysing the ways in which 'masculinity' is constructed in their own lives, and the ways in which this construction affects their interactions with and attitudes towards others.

This chapter is based on a study I conducted on young male adolescents' perceptions of masculinity (Martino 1998). I developed a set of criteria to construct profiles of boys aged between 12 and 13 years that were examples of particular types of masculinity. One hundred or so male students, aged 12–13 years, were asked to write an extended response that recorded their impressions of each profile. Students were also asked to indicate which profiled boy they related to the most and whether they knew of people at their school who might feel like any of the boys. Included here are four of these brief profiles, and some samples of the boys' responses to them.

The business of teaching

Historically, English lessons have always been in the business of shaping students as particular kinds of people. Teaching students to read in particular ways has always been linked by educators to processes of 'moral reflection' and possibilities of understanding their 'self' in relation to others and to the world (ie self-realisation). Ian Hunter (1988) argues that texts are used in literacy lessons in ways that encourage students to produce particular responses that accord with specific social norms or expectations, and whose 'acceptability' (or otherwise) is judged by the teacher.

This moral and 'normative' literacy work is a well recognised part of the so-called personal growth models of reading. However, the point I want to make is that self-reflection and self-problematisation are also part and parcel of critical literacy approaches to teaching children to read. In critical approaches to literacy, texts are used to promote reflection on social practices and the ways in which these practices impact on students' lives. For example, students can be engaged in moral self-reflection and in problematising the effects of certain cultural practices such as those that perpetuate racism or sexism.

I want to suggest that these self-reflective and self-problematising reading practices can be used to address issues relating to masculinity. These powerful and persuasive existing classroom reading practices can be put to use—subverted, if you like—to encourage students to reflect on dominant versions of masculinity, the ways in which these versions are used to police boundaries of so called acceptable behaviour, and the ways in which they themselves are implicated in this policing and/or its effects.

Boys at school: Four profiles

MILES

Miles was a very intelligent boy but he didn't like school and he definitely didn't like doing home work. It was all so boring. He would often just sit in class and daydream about football training and the game on the weekend that he always enjoyed playing. He could hardly ever be bothered listening to teachers because the work just didn't interest him. Sure, he liked reading but not all of the stuff that he had to read at school—it was just so boring. He liked reading sports and surf magazines, though, because he really enjoyed playing football and surfing with his friends. Because of this he had gained the reputation of being somewhat a *rebel*. He also loved writing but this was something that he kept very private. Sometimes he wrote about very personal things that he was afraid to share with anyone else. It also helped him to sort through what he was feeling. He didn't feel comfortable sharing these feelings with his friends although he sometimes talked to his mum when he was feeling down or angry about something. Besides, she always seemed to know what he was feeling.

JOEL

Joel was very quiet and he knew that people talked about him behind his back. Some of them even called him names. He somehow knew that he didn't quite fit and felt down about it—he didn't like playing sport, he didn't like the kinds of jokes that other boys would tell, the way they'd talk about girls, the way they'd boast about things at times to impress one another. In fact, when he thought about it that's what they always did, they'd just 'give everybody crap' to get a laugh from their mates. He would sometimes go to the library at lunchtime to escape the names they would call him. He felt lonely at times and wished that he could be like everybody else because then life would be so much easier for him, at school anyway. At the end of the day he didn't know whether he was really that different from everybody else or whether they had just made him feel he was different. After all, he had feelings like all other boys, didn't he? He liked listening to heavy metal music like many other boys, he liked going to the movies. But somehow he knew that he was different. Maybe it was because he loved painting and reading? He would spend hours reading and painting. Drawing pictures was something that he also enjoyed. In this way he was able to express what he felt. He would sometimes draw pictures which represented what he was feeling, but few people would really understand the significance of these drawings. He loved to draw pictures of flying dragons. They were so graceful, so strong and yet somehow so free. The sky was their limit. He loved to draw pictures of other lands which existed only in his imagination because in these worlds he could be free and he could choose to be who he wanted to be.

MARCO

Marco was scared and often felt depressed. No-one seemed to understand him and he had to pretend, cover up so many things almost all of the time. But it was the shame that was the worst thing. The way he had been made to feel so worthless for simply being who he was. At first there was this group of boys who would just follow him around and chant awful names at him. He was even too scared to go to the toilet for fear of what they might do to him. No-one had the right to persecute him or to make fun of him—to call him the kinds of names that they called him, to threaten him with violence. They made him feel like some kind of freak. Was he? They made him feel so ashamed and yet he was just who he was—a teenage boy growing up, learning about life and discovering things about himself. Without his friends, Alicia and Jessica, he didn't know how he would have survived at school. They stood up for him and supported him. There were just so many things that he couldn't understand or accept, so many feelings and thoughts churning around inside of him, so many questions but no answers, so many fears. Would he be able to accept what he might discover about himself? What might he discover about others? Would he have a place in the world? Would he be able to survive?

ANDREW

Andrew had a Chinese face but he was born in Australia. He had spent all of his life in this country. His parents were born in Malaysia and had worked hard to begin a new life in Australia. When Andrew was in Year 7, he remembered one teacher asking in class whether he had any problems with the English language. She needed to know so that she could help him to develop his writing skills. She also asked him how long he had been in Australia. He told her that he was born in Australia, spoke English very well and really didn't need any extra help. Andrew also felt that he couldn't win in a culture where he didn't seem to fit. When he went out with his Australian friends he felt that he was judged by other Asian people for betraying his own culture. And when he was with his Asian friends he often felt afraid and unsafe, a target for racial abuse. Somehow he had to find his place between two worlds or two cultures.

Analysing the boys' responses

Judging from their written responses, most of the boys involved in the study engaged thoughtfully with the four profiles and readily 'identified' with the character in each as though the characters were indeed real people who *reflected* aspects of the reader's true self.

Example 1: Jeremy

Jeremy's response highlights the extent to which the students' responses are effects of particular reading practices that require them to use the text to reflect on their own 'self' and their experiences:

JEREMY

> I think these boys were all having problems with life and their feelings. Often they were hiding their thoughts and emotions, in some ways, for different reasons. There was a wide range of characters there. Miles was an interesting one, a 'rebel' who was also intelligent. Joel and Marco were like victims, picked on, nervous and unable to fit in, with different thoughts and feelings. Andrew felt like he didn't belong, a target for racism in a sometimes cruel culture. I kind of relate to bits and pieces of those boys, not just one or two of them. I feel unsure and down sometimes like some of them, and things get hard for me too. I think some people in the school may feel like this; they are being teased, they are having family problems, peer pressure etc.

Jeremy is able to use the characters in the profiles to reflect on himself in this way because he has already been taught to do so. The self-realising, self-reflective reader who demonstrates a capacity for moral introspection appears to be the kind of reader that we are in the business of producing in the literacy classroom. Nevertheless, it still points towards the potential of this approach to reading for engaging boys in a literacy practice which makes analyses of masculinity its target.

Example 2: John

Like many of the students, John identified most closely with Miles:

JOHN

> I think I relate to Miles the most, because I do the same things as him. I'm not intelligent but I'm average at school and I don't like it. I also don't concentrate during class that much because I'm thinking about my basketball game or my tennis on Sunday. I am very good at sport and that's all I think about every day. I don't have a reputation as a rebel like Miles but I am considered a very good sportsman by everyone else. I also don't share my feelings with my friends because I'm afraid I'll get a bad reputation because no other boys talk about their feelings. I also can't talk my feelings to my mum because I don't have a relationship with my mum or dad.

Miles reflected a particular 'mainstream', and therefore desired, form of heterosexual masculinity. Many of the boys appeared to identify with particular social practices and attitudes that have become associated with this particular form of masculinity. For example, they seem to align themselves closely with Miles because he finds school boring and would rather play or think about sport. This alignment seems to occur despite Miles' comments about his private writing practices. Engaging in personal writing does not appear to be consistent with acting out a tough macho masculinity in dominant Australian culture (see Martino 1994). In this respect, there appears to be a space created here to challenge or suggest additions to certain social practices which are generally prized by boys acting out their version of masculinity at school.

Example 3: Rory and Shaun

Although most boys tended to empathise with Joel and Marco, others produced quite derogatory and seemingly homophobic readings of these characters:

RORY

> Well when you only have GIRLS as friends, you got some serious problems. That's why he was made to feel ashamed because he's a poofter.

SHAUN

> I think Marco is a real faggot, he hangs around with girls, no other boys like him, they make him feel like a freak because he is one. His friend Alicia and Jessica have to stick up for him because he's weak, what a loser!

Here, the boys' use of language highlights the social forces at play as they learn to define their masculinity. For instance, both Shaun and Rory label Marco 'a real faggot' or 'poofter' because he hangs around with girls rather than boys. Because Marco associates with girls, his masculinity is immediately brought into question with his sexuality coming under fire. Not only is being a 'poofter' associated with being feminine, it is also tied to being weak and being a 'loser'—to having no power.

Example 4: Adam

Many of the responses, however, also indicate the extent to which the boys—at least on a private level—are able to reject public displays of a particular kind of 'macho' masculinity. In fact, a number of the participating students disapproved of Miles. For example:

ADAM

> I think Miles is a pretty ignorant person. If he wants to learn he has to stop ignoring things and take things as they come. I think he will feel left out in a sense because he likes to be different. I think people would regard him as a very selfish person.

Example 5: Anthony and Steve

Other boys focused on their experiences of racism to identify with both Joel and Andrew:

ANTHONY
> I choose Joel and Andrew because I find most in common with those two, Andrew especially. The only difference is I don't dislike the way the guys talk, I only get pee'd off when it leads to me. Mainly about my racial background and general chunkiness. That's where I can relate to Andrew. I feel I can't get anywhere in a different culture. Like they could always just call me a 'gook' or a 'nip' whenever they want to and I can't do anything, calling them racists doesn't help because suddenly racism is 'cool' now.

Here Anthony links racist name-calling practices to being 'cool'. Racist labelling and name calling function, on occasions, as means by which some boys are able to enact an abusive form of masculinity. Racist practices may very well be tied to a peer group dynamics in which cruel taunts and send-ups become identifiable instances of establishing a dominant, white, heterosexual masculinity. For example:

STEVE
> Andrew just has to find out who his real friends are and stick with them either black, yellow or white. Once he finds his real friends, then he will be set for life. Real friends will stand by each other. He should not feel bad about betraying his culture. I'm German, my dad's German, my mum's an Aussie. I get people calling me natzi [sic] boy and writing these symbols on their hand. I guess it annoys me but I'm used to it.

Steve's reference to being called a 'natzi' says much about the ways in which boys learn to relate to one another in peer group situations and the role that racist practices might have to play in acting out their masculinity on certain occasions. Steve is one of many of the boys participating in this study who indicated a strong disapproval of the racist practices mentioned by Anthony.

Some dangers

I want to emphasise that, while some students produced homophobic and racist responses, many were willing to question the social practices of their peers. They rejected the name calling and believed that individuals should not be 'put down'. Many boys were also able to critically reflect on what it meant to act 'cool' and rejected the abusive practices which were often related to behaving in this way. On the basis of this research, it would appear that these students have already developed quite sophisticated capacities for self-reflection and moral introspection. It is in this sense that I believe teachers who are interested in social justice can draw on already existing techniques and training to engage their students to reflect critically on masculinity. Whether students willingly accept the norms that are built into this critical literacy practice is another issue.

There are definite possibilities for the teacher-as-researcher to use the techniques of self-reflection as a scaffold for preparing students to critically question masculinity. However, as Pam Gilbert (1990) has already pointed out, such techniques can lead to authorising homophobic, racist and misogynist readings. It may be necessary to restrict the use of such reading practices; for example, teachers-as-researchers could privately undertake an audit, similar to the process I describe in this chapter, of the range of reading positions adopted by their students in response to a particular text. This knowledge may then be used strategically in helping teachers to prepare effective critical literacy units of work for their classrooms. For me, despite the dangers involved, teachers should find ways of placing masculinity on the agenda, and create opportunities for their students to challenge particular gender regimes in which masculinity is defined in opposition to femininity.

Devising classroom strategies

It is possible to argue that already available techniques for reading texts can be used effectively to establish ground from which to target the social construction of masculinities. Once students have responded to a text in a self-reflexive way, they need to be encouraged to think in more explicit terms about masculinity and to challenge the ways in which some people choose to define it and act it out. The following activities are not provided as a definitive model, but it is hoped that they will gesture towards what a critical literacy practice, designed to target masculinity, might look like.

Some sample activities

In small groups write your own definition of the word 'masculinity'. Can you explain what you think 'being masculine' means?

Men are often presented in magazines and advertisements in different ways. Find as many different pictures of men as you can. You must be able to explain what the differences are.

One student made the following comment about Joel:

'Joel is a loser because he doesn't do boys' things!'

Do you consider this to be a fair comment? Discuss what you would consider to be 'boys' things'? What are some of the things that boys are expected to do?

If boys do not meet these expectations, do you think it is fair that they should be labelled with certain names?

Role play a situation in which a boy chooses not to do what boys are expected to do but is still accepted and well liked by his friends.

'Marco is a real faggot because he hangs around with girls.'

Do you consider this to be a fair comment? Does having girls as friends necessarily mean that a boy is gay? Sometimes people can be discriminated against, teased and even bashed because they are considered to be, or are gay. How do you think this problem might best be addressed in schools so that all students can be treated fairly and with respect?

In small groups write a comic strip which involves what teachers and students in schools can to do to address the problem of name calling and bullying.

Conclusion

The point I want to re-emphasise here is that activities like these can be used within existing frameworks for teaching reading to help students develop capacities for interrogating masculinities. The profiles I constructed (six in total) have already proved useful in initially engaging students in this kind of practice by encouraging them to become self-reflective about the ways in which many boys learn to relate to, and are expected to behave towards others. More importantly, by using this practice in the first instance, the teacher-as-researcher can do some ground work and learn more about the attitudes and cultural background of her or his students. This will assist teachers to devise suitable activities which encourage students to interrogate and challenge restrictive practices of masculinities in specific and hopefully enacted ways.

NOTE

I would like to thank my doctoral supervisor, Annette Patterson, and Bronwyn Mellor for helping me to develop these understandings about reading practices. Thanks also to Michele Knobel and Eileen Honan for their editorial input.

References

Butler, J. (1996). 'The poof paradox: Homonegativity and silencing in three Hobart high schools'. In L Laskey and C Beavis (eds) *Schooling and Sexualities: Teaching for a Positive Sexuality*, Geelong: Deakin University for Education and Change.

Connell, R W (1989) 'Cool guys, swots and wimps: The interplay of masculinity and education', *Oxford Review of Education*. Vol 15, No 3, pp 291–303.

Connell, R W (1995) *Masculinities*. Sydney: Allen and Unwin.

Epstein, D (1997) 'Boyz' own stories: Masculinities and sexualities in schools', *Gender and Education*. Vol 9, No 1, pp 105–115.

Gilbert, P (1990) 'Authorizing disadvantage: Authorship and creativity in the language classroom'. In F. Christie (ed) *Literacy for a Changing World*. Hawthorn: ACER.

Hunter, I (1988) *Culture and Government: The Emergence of Literary Education*. London: Macmillan Press.

Jordan, E (1995) 'Fighting boys and fantasy play: The construction of masculinity in the early years of school', *Gender and Education*. Vol 7, No 1, pp 69–86.

Kehily, M and Nayak, A (1997) '"Lads and laughter": Humour and the production of heterosexual hierarchies', *Gender and Education*. Vol 9, No 1, pp 69–87.

Mac an Ghaill, M (1994) *The Making of Men: Masculinities, Sexualities and Schooling*. Buckingham and Philadelphia: Open University Press.

Martino, W (1994) 'Masculinity and learning: Exploring boys' underachievement and under-representation in subject English', *Interpretations*. Vol 27, No 2, pp 22–57.

Martino, W (1997) '"A bunch of arseholes": Exploring the politics of masculinity for adolescent boys in schools', *Social Alternatives*. Vol 16, No 3, July, pp 39–43.

Martino, W (1998) 'Interrogating Masculinities: Regimes of Practice'. Unpublished doctoral thesis, School of Education, Murdoch University, Melbourne.

Nayak, A and Kehily, M (1996) 'Playing it straight: Masculinities, homophobias and schooling', *Journal of Gender Studies*. Vol 5, No 2, pp 211–230.

Parker, A (1996) 'The construction of masculinity within boys' physical education', *Gender and Education*. Vol 8, No 2, pp 114–157.

Walker, J (1988) *Louts and Legends: Male Youth Culture in an Inner-City School*. Sydney, London and Boston: Allen and Unwin.

CHAPTER 7

Words and life: Critical literacy and cultural action

CHRIS SEARLE WITH MICHELE KNOBEL

Chris Searle's approach to critical literacy focuses on social action, and in this chapter he describes his work with diverse, multicultural groups of students from economically disadvantaged areas in England. Searle presents the key operating principles that drive his approach to critical literacy and provides an overview of his approach to critical teaching that is supported by examples of specific classroom practices and texts produced by his students. Searle explains that he encourages his students to use their literary skills to help bring out real social changes to the inequalities that pervade their lives.

As a boy, I was schooled during the end days of British imperialism. The Suez Canal was 'taken from us' by Nasser in 1956 when I was in my first year of secondary modern school, and dozens of African and Caribbean colonies claimed independence in the following years. Nevertheless, the inheritance of the Empire was still strong; the red colour marking British territories and colonies stood out on the world atlases we used at school, and the children's fiction available in the school library glorified imperialism. Indeed, the words of Lord Meath, the founder of Empire Day in England, were still thematic: that the British must still prove to be 'a Spartan-like, virile race . . . worthy to bear the white man's burden and not be afraid' (in Auden 1956). I was one of 'Britannia's children'—although possibly the last generation to be truly so—acculturated to the 'strong and lofty imperialism' (ibid) of the British Empire and educated with textbooks, periodicals and Biggles-type fiction (not to mention the private school world of Billy Bunter and Hurree Jamset Ram Singh). In these ways, and many more besides, I was thoroughly and truly immersed in a particular version of my relationship with, and role within, an imperial world and its dominance over the 'imperial races' who peopled much of it.

I mention this because I want to make it clear that young English people like myself were systematically indoctrinated into a highly partial view (in favour of the white 'races' and upper classes) by means of our schooling. I wanted to preface this chapter with this observation because I have been accused many times of 'indoctrinating' students into a particular view of the world—a criticism regularly aimed at critical literacy teachers in general (see Searle 1998). This kind of plaint, however, assumes teachers' attitudes to the body of knowledge they transmit to their students, and the methods they use to transmit it, are, or should be, always necessarily impartial, neutral, and certainly *not* 'ideological'. However, those who claim the right to assert that teaching is a neutral and always objective enterprise promote their own position as a kind of pre-given baseline for judging what is 'educational truth' and therefore what is the normal state of affairs, and what is not. This is an ideological stance on their part; and all too often it is a stance against 'classroom ideas and practices that question the ways power, wealth, status, opportunities and life chances, adequate housing, dignity, academic achievement, and many other social goods are currently allocated—and that question the bases on which these allocations are made' (Lankshear 1998).

In what follows, I describe the ways in which my students and I have challenged educational and social norms that worked in the main to disadvantage working-class students and their families. In doing so, I present key operating principles that have driven my critical literacy work with students over the years, an overview of my general pedagogical approach, and examples of classroom practice where students and teachers in schools designated as 'disadvantaged' have not only questioned inequalities and injustices, but have acted on the outcomes to their questioning in ways that have, in many cases, brought about significant cultural and social changes in their own lives and in the lives of others. Although the examples I present are taken from students who are generally in their first years of secondary schooling, there is much here, I am sure, that will suggest possibilities for critical literacy practices in primary school classrooms in Australia and New Zealand.

Key operating principles

1 Imagination

Imagination has always played a central role in my approach to teaching. The imagination in teaching is the great motivator; it stretches the mind, provokes engagement in learning and encourages empathy and human understanding. In my experience, schooling has regularly diminished, and even removed, the influence of the imagination in teaching and literacy learning (see Searle 1998 on this creative–critical principle). In my own teaching, I have worked at re-establishing the imagination as integral to students' learning. For me, this entails what I call 'imaginative empathy', whereby students—with the help of stimulus, information and insights garnered from poetry, plays, letters, interviews, speeches, movies, and other texts—imagine themselves in informed ways into the lives of others. Thus, in my classes, writing literary pieces (eg narratives, poems, diary entries) isn't simply a literacy exercise, but is indissolubly part of the process of knowing.

For example, in the poem that follows, a ten-year-old boy from a Sheffield primary school considers literacy—and, in particular, the tool of writing and language: the pencil—from the imagined perspective of an Ethiopian school student who has taken part in his nation's mass literacy campaign by teaching illiterate adults within his own family. In analysing literacy learning by means of imaginative empathy and capturing this empathy in words, Joe signals his growing understanding of the functions of literacy in his own life, as well as in another life thousands of miles away (see also Searle 1993). At the same time, he is expanding and refining his creative and evocative use of words and ideas.

IT'S ONLY A PENCIL

Here I am looking at something that holds my whole life.
If I let it go my life will be gone.
Not only my life, but my family's life as well.
But who cares? After all, it's only a pencil.

It's only a pencil, but look what I can do with it.
I can write a letter for help with it.
I can learn at school with it.
I can teach my family with it –
If only we had more pencils and less guns.

Joe[1]

And it doesn't stop there—he is also an active part of a mass campaign of British young people raising funds and resources for the Ethiopian literacy movement.

2 Students must become proficient users of standard English

A second principle that guides my teaching is an insistence that working-class children are provided with ample opportunity to become proficient users of standard English. It is imperative that working class children should learn to read, write, spell, punctuate and to develop the word as a tool and as a weapon in their inevitable struggles for improvement and liberation. This means an understanding of basic grammar and sentence analysis, the power to spell correctly and to use punctuation effectively, to know and be able to construct myriad figures of speech, and to be able to write sequentially and coolly while maintaining creative strength and imaginative energy. In short, critical literacy can only become the basis of a genuinely critical and interventionist foundation for life and action if it successfully brings the student into the world by means of written, spoken, poeticised, analytical, cognitive, and affective language processes and genres. This foundation also requires that students have access to a social and personal language that is strong and confident enough to challenge, struggle with, and change the personal and political problems that face urban young people at the tip of our century.

3 Promoting language pride

In tandem with promoting standard English excellence, a third principle to which I subscribe is 'language pride'; that is, student pride in every language, dialect or language variant that they speak. Thus, for example, providing spaces in class for students to compose and present texts in a language or dialect of their choosing[2], giving students opportunities to reflect on the effects of living in a linguistically diverse community, and so on, become important. These kinds of experiences enable students in my classes to produce texts like the following[3]:

LANGUAGE

Speak the language you were born with,
Show your feelings to the people around you.
Show the people you are proud of your language,
Language is a great thing.
With language you can make friends.
People will know you as long as you live,
Language can help you to understand things around you
Language can make you proud and happy,
Language will lead you to happiness.
Don't let anyone make fun of your language
Shout your language out to the people around you!
Let them know that you love your language
And you will speak your language as long as you live.
So shout your language out!

Izat[4] (a Panjabi/English speaker)

(EXCERPT FROM) BACK IN THEM DAYS

Back in them days
my Nan dint 'ave no messing about.
A quick clip dint do no 'arm,
And it also taught 'em a lesson.

My muvver and 'er bruvver were always up
to somert,
Climbin' trees, scratchin' knees,
And they always asked wiv a please.

Lee (South Yorkshire/English speaker)

In my mind, coupling (a) each student's ability to use languages and dialects to freely express themselves with (b) a working understanding of the rules of the languages we use, forms a basic objective of critical literacy.

4 Situated pedagogy

A fourth principle driving my teaching is 'situated pedagogy'; that is, curriculum content and approaches are not dictated and bounded strictly by syllabus documents and national curriculum statements, but grounded in the local community, and in local issues and events (which, given the multiculturalism of many British cities necessarily embraces larger issues and events). I have found repeatedly that even reluctant readers and writers will engage in projects that have direct bearing on their interests, concerns and lives. In a very real sense I have always tried to make the relationships between words and the world explicit to students.

5 Language and action

This leads to a fifth principle operating in my approach to teaching: language and action. In my teaching the two have become inseparable. A vocal and public critic of my work—one of the governors of a school in which I was working—once argued vehemently that poetry in the classroom should not be 'deliberate social comment' but more an activity of fun. However, I believe that poetry is both. To deny the potential poetry has to touch the lives of readers and listeners is to overlook the historical role of poetry in commenting upon social events and situations, and in stirring people to action. Consequently, I refuse to renege on my commitment to developing students' critical literacy techniques and tools via poetry and other literary texts. Indeed, this principle of language and action is enacted in a cyclic process of dialogue, reflection and action in every critical literacy project I work on with students and others (see also Freire 1974). This is demonstrated in the projects I describe later.

6 Mutuality

Finally, the sixth principle to which I subscribe is 'mutuality'. I have never taught without learning, and believe that there can be no true teaching without the teacher also learning. From Stepney, East London, to Tobago and Grenada in the Caribbean, from Nampula in Mozambique to Fir Vale in Sheffield, my students and their communities have always been my teachers. This principle of mutuality extends to sharing my students' and their communities' struggles for better lives, and plays itself out in critical literacy projects that bring about real social changes. But I am getting ahead of myself. First I want to describe my pedagogical approach to developing students' literacy *and* critical literacy skills and strategies.

Pedagogical approach

Certain fundamental phases characterise my approach to teaching critical literacy and expressive writing. For simplicity's sake, and by way of creating a mnemonic, I describe each of the seven phases with a word beginning with the letter 'C': Creation, Consideration, Consciousness,

Collaboration, Confidence, Cross-over and Cultural action. These phases overlap, and their 'order' is fluid, according to the kind of critical literacy project we are undertaking. Nevertheless, one way or another, each phase or process is found in my classroom critical literacy curricula.

1 Creation

The act of creation involves the mobilisation of words and the imagination in response to a certain situation—selected by the teacher, students, or by both—and discussed in class. Each theme, event, or issue is usually introduced to students by combining the three or sometimes four classes for the year level being taught. The purpose of this combined session is to provide students with information usually by means of poems, narratives, plays, novels, extracts, handouts, and commentaries and questions from students and staff. At different times, these introductory sessions also include a relevant documentary or movie, guest speakers or performers (eg poets, novelists, musicians, cricketers, actors and the like), and readings from biographies, memoirs and other historical documents collected by teachers from libraries and other archives. This introductory session is followed often by breaking into separate classes, and then into smaller groups comprising two to four students in each. These student groups foster creativity by providing opportunities for students to engage with a range of reference materials and in imagination-based activities as they produce their texts. We teachers invariably learn much in this process, too, and the teaching–learning relationships in these projects tend in the main to be side-by-side interactions as well as face-to-face.

The outcome of this phase is the creation of new or reworked patterns of language, poetical thoughts, configurations of words and images that are forged by an individual, a pair or a group who are enlarging the situation they are considering by treating it with empathy and imagining themselves into different world views.

2 Consideration

Creative activity is consolidated by reflection and the consideration of events or issues by means of individual and collective thinking about the new work on the page. This may involve one student reading work-in-progress to a group, which provides feedback on how the words made them feel and what sorts of images the words invoked. This feedback extends to editorial comment and advice on grammatical structure, word choice, spelling and the like. At other times, consideration may be enacted in the form of the teacher and student working on the rhythm of a text, spelling accuracy, visual images and so forth.

3 Consciousness

Acts of creation and consideration generally lead to the beginnings of a new or revised consciousness; that is, new or revised ways of understanding the world. I want to make very clear here that this is never a process of indoctrination. Even though I always make my own stance on an issue clear to students, they are encouraged to question and challenge my position and construct their own informed perspectives. In addition, the variety of resources brought into the classroom or examined in the community provide plenty of scope for students to experiment with language as a vehicle for expressing their fears, hates, loves, joys, pride in certain things, and so on. For example, the following excerpt from a recount is grounded unquestionably in this student's lived experience, rather than in her teacher's everyday life:

> . . . 'Hey you Paki!' he shouted.
> I felt sick at his ignorance. These people didn't even know the difference between Pakistani and Arab people.
>
> Nahda[5]

In addition, community members are involved regularly in enriching students' understandings of their world. I well remember the time a local professional photographer, whose photographic themes resonated with the poetic themes my students were engaging with at that time, worked with us. He took copies of some of the students' poems and superimposed the their words across poster-size blow-ups of photographs which seemed to be making similar statements. These images included close-ups of old people, a boy kicking a football across a stretch of waste ground, a young Asian girl photographed against a wall of brick and rubble. When he brought these images into my class, we used them as prompts for students' to identify with the people in the photographs and to imagine their lives and realities, and to express their ideas and feelings in words. For example, this includes poetic statements like the following:

> Racism is like a word chucked out of hell –
> if hell can't cope with this word,
> How will we on Earth?
>
> Ghulam[6]

This word and image work became a stimulus for further poems and expressive writing, resulting in professionally published poetry anthologies such as *Stepney Words, School of the World*, and *Heart of Sheffield*.

At other times, I would take my class for walks along the streets and to the parks, squares and churchyards of the local area, getting them to bring their exercise books to record their observations, sketch images, and draft lines that they can later incorporate into descriptive passages and poems. On these field trips, I always ask students to look at the world immediately around them, at the local people in the streets, and at the houses and council estates close to the school, enacting the words of William Blake: 'My streets are my ideas of imagination'. These are people and scenes that these students see everyday, but they are asked to look at them in new ways, to study them closely, to invent metaphors and similes to describe them, and to treat what they see with imaginative empathy.

4 Collaboration

Opportunities for students to work collaboratively with peers and their teacher are maximised in my classes. This collaboration takes the form of pairs or small groups working on aspects of a larger project that involves the whole class, or it may be that individual work spurs a student into forming a group to investigate an aspect of an issue or event in more detail. This can include asking a peer to interview a member of the community in another language and translating it for the student who is interested in what is being said, but who cannot speak the language; or students working together to turn an interview text into a poem or biographical text. In addition, collaboration may occur spontaneously around an almost-finished piece of work when students once again consider and offer feedback on the competence and eloquence of the text. Indeed, I have always found that students appear to experience a real sense of social engagement when they read and comment on the work of their classmates.

5 Confidence

The products of the literate imagination generate increased confidence, both in the self and in others—teachers and community members included—working on the same or similar projects. Students begin to see and reflect on their expressive and literate capabilities and often realise for the first time in their lives that they *do* have something to say and are able to say it in ways that reach out to others. This deliberate emphasis on enhancing students' confidence is underscored by our practice of suspending words or phrases from students' poems on walls, sewing them on banners, reading them out in school assemblies and community meetings, and sharing them as messages of achievement in published books—always giving these words, phrases and poems back to those who owned them as a form of respect and recognition of the writers and what they have written. Throughout my teaching career I have worked to have students' expressive writing published; but not in the all too conventional format of labouriously wordprocessed texts with pre-packaged page borders and graphics, that are printed out and glued into exercise books or Blu-Tacked to walls. Rather, students' texts are published professionally as paperback, glossy-covered anthologies copyrighted to the school or to a community organisation, with individuals retaining the copyright to their own texts.

6 Cross-over

Working in a linguistically diverse classroom where cultural symbols and narrative genres are broad and different, the cross-over of culture becomes an emphatic objective of literacy development and critical pedagogy. Cultures and languages can be shared and exchanged by means of imagination;

that is, through informed empathy the others become oneself and oneself becomes others (along with all of the 'humanness' this necessarily entails). This kind of cultural cross-over generates human solidarity that crosses cultural borders. New ways of learning about the world are arrived at by means of an 'embodied' imagination that has the capacity to *become* other humans in far-flung situations. For example, Sallie, a white, working class girl living in Sheffield, writes about black youth resisting apartheid in Soweto townships[7]:

IMMORTAL

They'll live forever
And never die
They're joined to us
More often than ever.
We breathe for them,
Fight for them,
Live for them
We are them.

Sallie

7 Cultural action

Repeatedly, for many of my students over the years, imaginative acts have become cultural and social acts. The processes of creation and collaboration, fused with (usually) new-found self-confidence and modes of expression, and the use of meaningful themes and content, often mobilise students to bring about real social changes in their school and community. My point here is explained best by means of an example. One of the most potent occurred in response to a story in a local newspaper about a toddler picking up a discarded syringe on a plot of waste ground near the school, playing with it and putting it in her mouth while her horrified mother ran to her to remove it. This had a strong effect on the class, and resonated with an earlier event where a 15-year-old boy had passed out in the school lunch room after downing a dangerous concoction of drugs in a street near the school earlier in the day. One girl, 11-year-old Sarah, wrote:

THE SYRINGE

I am the syringe
that you find in the street.
I am the syringe
that attacks you on the waste ground.
I am the syringe
that pricks and kills you.
I am the syringe
that you should stay away from.

> I am like a live snake
> that gives you a bite.
> I am like a live wire
> that gives you a shock.
> Stay away!
> Or else you will have
> a very short time to live!
>
> What does it feel like
> When you leave your child standing
> on waste ground? And I prick her –
> What would you do
> When your child is infected?
> What would you do?
>
> Sarah

This became a theme poem for the school's anti-drug work. It was read out in assemblies, studied in classes, published and performed, too, by its young author at city-wide events. This poem is writing at its most starkly creative, but also at its most concrete; connected to real life and a campaign to oppose a serious and growing problem.

The many projects in which my students and I have been involved are an ongoing testament to the power of empathetic imagination and eloquent written expression when used as a catalyst for real cultural action. Some of these projects are described briefly below.

Projects

I would dearly love to go into describing the details of the critical literacy projects in which my students and I have participated. However, I only have room for cursory listings of what we did. I won't pretend that implementing these projects has been hassle free, or has been blessed unconditionally by the managers, or governors, of the schools in which I have taught, or even by local education authorities. Nevertheless, my approach to critical literacy has always had the unreserved support of my students, their parents, and even the wider local community. For example, the *Stepney Words* project in an East London school mentioned earlier was widely supported by students, their parents, and even the local community, but not by the school's governors, who claimed the 'everyday-ness' of the students' poems—written in response to what they saw around them—were too bleak and drab.

> I live on my own
> In a cold damp room
> No one to talk to
> No one to see
>
> My children are married
> They live far away
> My husband died
> On a cold winter's day
>
> Tina

> I come from Stepney, lived here all me life
> Loads of cheap markets
> Bargains at half price
> Jumpers and skirts, trousers cheap
> All muddled up in any old heap
> Dirty old women, shouting out their wares
> Everybody stinks, nobody cares
> All dirty, greasy things bunged into bins
> Stinkin' rotten hole is Stepney
>
> Diane

The governors suggested the students should begin again, rewriting these poems using more 'cheerful cockney sparrow' themes. Despite this criticism, we pressed ahead with the students' original poems and the anthology was funded and published as *Stepney Words* by the local community. The students' poems created a mix of national furore and acclaim, and my decision to forge ahead initially lost me my teaching position. Yet, the students and their parents responded by taking strike action for my reinstatement. For me, the strike was clear evidence that the students had seen the governors' reluctance to publish their poems as a political and cultural attack on their achievement, as well as on their right to publicly express their opinions about the area in which they lived. Moreover, the cultural action taken by these students was embedded deeply in their motivation and abilities to *write*, and not just read; and in their commitment to becoming (critically) literate in order to more fully and consciously understand and begin to change the world around them.

Other projects resulting in cultural action included working with school parents in Brixton, South London, to campaign for improved council housing. In this particular case, whole blocks of flats were left without heating during the winter, and families were suffering health-wise due to their damp and cold living conditions. As a teacher at a local primary school close to these housing blocks, I became aware of these conditions through my students who frequently came to school tired and cold, complaining of another sleepless night. As the weather turned to winter, my ten-year-old students voiced their unhappiness over the dangerously unstable paraffin stoves their parents used for heating in the damp conditions of their flats. These stoves themselves became health risks, with one serious fire after another. The teachers at this school felt we should be assisting parents directly, not only helping them with their campaign, but also with trying to draw widespread public attention to the dangers and oppressions that took a central position in our students' lives.

With my class, I began by asking students to tell in poetic form how they felt about what was happening in their lives. The paraffin stoves, their dangers and the accidents they caused, kept re-occurring in the students' poems, and I decided to write a play with the paraffin stoves fires and tenants' resistance to the conditions that caused them as the main themes. In these students' lives outside school, their parents were occupying local government offices in order to have their voices heard, a tenants' action group had been formed, and a rent strike for proper heating facilities had begun. It was important to me that the curriculum respond to the exigencies of the lives of my students, affirming and giving strength to their parents' actions. Accordingly, the play dramatised students' responses to the fires and their parents' protests, while simultaneously underlining and celebrating the internationalism of the school. Students spoke in their own particular languages and dialects, and the play took its incidents from local events narrated during classroom discussions. The play was performed in the classroom and to the rest of the school, and later at a Tenants' Action Group meeting at a local church hall. I then rewrote the play script as a children's book, beautifully illustrated by a teaching colleague. It was published with the title *Ferndale Fires* (after the name of the large block of flats adjacent to the school).

Ferndale Fires was intended to be a curriculum project of cultural action, and it proved to be so, drawing together the work of the classroom with a particular struggle involving the students and their families outside the school. In this way, the local community *became* the curriculum. This writing and reading project contrasted starkly with the developmentally graded books used in schools at that time to teach students to read. In these 'Peter and Jane' (Ladybird series) books, the two middle-class, young white protagonists move in a world of neat suburban housing, private cars, red setter dogs, holidays by the seaside and rich relatives like Mr White, who lives in a large country house. This clean, safe world also includes friendly policemen: 'I like the police,' says Peter. 'They help you.' The world of these books was entirely alien to the lives of my students. *Ferndale Fires*—the play and the book—sought to reflect students' own worlds, and in doing so, exchange alienating reading experiences for authentic ones, pen-and-ink children for flesh-and-blood ones.

The writing project that culminated in the publication of a poetry anthology, titled *Classrooms of Resistance*, was a direct response to and critique of the commercial redevelopment of local docklands and the subsequent loss of low-rent housing, and the closure of the local hospital. This project also encompassed international issues, including massacres and anti-apartheid resistance in South Africa, the fascist coup in Chile, and the repression of Catholic students by British soldiers in Belfast. My aim was to contextualise students' learning by grounding it in dynamic situations where struggle, resistance and change were in progress. For example, preliminary work gave a group of 11-year-old students the confidence to walk into the luxurious new Tower Hotel, built near the school, and ask for the hotel's list of tariffs. They brought this list to school and as a class we analysed room prices and other details listed about this hotel before writing about it.

RICH LUXURIES

Why did Taylor Walker build the hotel?
When there are so many people who have nowhere to dwell?
The Tower Hotel is only for millionaires
There is nowhere for us to live or to play.
In the Tower hotel they have waitresses
Where we have to slave for ourselves,
They have luxuries galore
Our homes are just a bore
They have 836 rooms in the hotel
Where we are scambled up in four.

Lynn

Poems such as this contradicted our critics in the media who claimed that children cannot think for themselves or respond to events through action unless they are led by an adult 'pied piper' or 'indoctrinator'. However, without prompting, students began naming the ubiquitous 'they' who controlled their parents' and their own lives, and to protest against the gross injustices being enacted on their very doorsteps.

There is room for only one more brief description, this time the project that resulted in the publication, *Lives of Love and Hope: A Sheffield Herstory*. This collection of recounts and poems celebrate the histories (or herstories) of the mothers of Earl Marshal school students in Sheffield. The students interviewed their mothers, grandmothers, or aunts—usually in their 'mother tongue'—and translated these interviews into English. These translations were then written up as recounts, edited and polished, then conferenced with peers and their teacher, and re-edited, before a final draft was produced. The resulting anthology documented family and cultural histories, as well as larger histories in the form of civil war, resistance movements, the mass movement of whole peoples, migration, racism and struggles in an adopted country (see also Searle 1998).

Other projects addressed include the Gulf War and the issues this generated for Arab, Yemeni and Pakistani students and families at the school;

the coma of a young Bengali man, Quddus Ali, induced by a racist beating and street terrorism from a group of young white fascist males, and made worse by the explicit inaction of local police; the war in Bosnia, the atrocities enacted in its name, and inter-racial conflict within the school and its community; and the literary documentation of family migration to England and of students' journeys to their parents' homelands.

Conclusion

The issues of inner-city education will never be resolved while we look upon these remarkable and vibrant students as problems. Many students I have taught in English working-class areas know and can negotiate in various ways at least two languages and two cultures by the age of 12 or 13. Accordingly, they often come to school knowing already how to analyse a social or cultural practice into its component features and processes. They are often much more world-aware than most of the people who criticise them, who describe them as 'lacking' or as a 'problem', and who hand them their curriculum prescriptions. My critical literacy work with these students over the years has taught me that effective literacy learning is forged in the heat of analysing and addressing real problems in these students' lives—problems that impact at the local level, but that may have been generated by events in other countries into which students imagine themselves with empathy.

Critical pedagogy can only be a credible pedagogy if it extends and enlarges the powers of language of the students and gives them the opportunity and ability to be in full control of all the words they need to challenge and act on inequitable social practices. Another 11-year-old student, Tabassum, eloquently captures our shared hope:

> One day
> a tree will grow high and strong
> in the garden of justice
> And live forever.

ENDNOTES

1. From Searle, C. (1998) *None But Our Words: Empowering Words, Empowering Lives.*
2. This usually occurs when work is presented to parents, or when a teacher involved in a presentation or classroom activity is reasonably fluent in the student's first or home language.
3. From *Valley of Words: Writings From Earl Marshal School, Sheffield*, 1992. Sheffield: Earl Marshal School.
4. Izat wrote fluently in English and Urdu and speaks fluently in English and Punjabi. He died only a few months after writing this poem. He had a weak heart and had been under hospital care for most of his short life. In Izat's memory, his classmates helped the textile teacher make a beautiful banner, which still hangs in the main resource area of the school. Over a picture of Izat, his name and the dates of his birth and death, is the boldly lettered line from his poem: SHOW THE PEOPLE YOU ARE PROUD OF YOUR LANGUAGE!

5. From *Valley of Words: Writings From Earl Marshal School, Sheffield*, 1992. Sheffield: Earl Marshal School.
6. From Searle, C. (1990) ed. *Freedom Children: A Tribute in Poetry to the Young People of South Africa from the Young People of Sheffield*. Sheffield: Sheffield City Council.
7. From Searle, C. (1990) ed. *Freedom Children: A Tribute in Poetry to the Young People of South Africa from the Young People of Sheffield*. Sheffield: Sheffield City Council.

References

Auden, W (1979) *Making, Knowing and Judging*. London: Clarendon Press.

Freire, P (1974) *Education: The Practice of Freedom*. London: Writers and Readers Cooperative.

Lankshear, C (1998) Foreword to C Searle, *None But Our Words: Empowering Words, Empowering Lives*. Buckingham: Open University Press, pp vii–xv.

Searle, C (1993) 'Words to a life-land: Literacy, the imagination, and Palestine'. In C Lankshear and P McLaren (eds) *Critical Literacy: Politics, Praxis, and the Postmodern*. New York: State University of New York Press, pp 167–191.

Searle, C (1997) *Living Community, Living School*. London: Tufell Press.

Searle, C (1998) *None But Our Word: Empowering Words, Empowering Lives*. Buckingham: Open University Press.

CHAPTER 8

Critical literacies in teacher education

MICHELE KNOBEL

In this chapter, Michele Knobel presents some of the activities, questions, and resources she uses with teacher education students to explore the meaning and application of critical literacy in primary classrooms. Her approach has two strands: one is aimed at developing beginning teachers' professional understanding of critical literacy as a concept and practice; the other aims at modelling possible approaches to critical literacy in the classroom.

Critical literacy is a major curriculum approach in many Australian states. Aside from its current educational trendiness, it is important for teachers and student teachers to *understand* what critical literacy is and *how it works* in classrooms—and elsewhere. This belief is grounded in my strong conviction that teachers are—or should be—agents of social change.

Consequently, this chapter builds on the theoretical and practical work of preceding chapters to present a do-it-yourself professional development base on which you can build and consolidate your understandings of critical literacy. This chapter comprises three main sections, and each section is headed with a 'key question' that can be used to direct your thinking or to generate a summary of the main points made in each section. As with most learning, it's likely you'll gain more from this chapter if you work through it as part of pair or as a member of a small group. The ideas and activities in this chapter are among those I use to encourage and develop the critical literacy understandings of undergraduate Bachelor of Education and Graduate Diploma of Education (Primary) students at the Queensland University of Technology (QUT). Including these ideas and activities here may also give practising teachers and other teacher educators insight into some of the processes for developing critical literacy understandings in primary teacher education at QUT.

In terms of prior reading and understanding on the reader's part, it is assumed that you have read the preceding chapters in this book. You may also want to revisit chapter 1 and the Glossary before reading further.

Conceptualising critical literacy

> **KEY QUESTION**
> What *is* critical literacy, and what is its role in your classroom?

Unfortunately, critical literacy is a much contested term and practice. The following list of 'takes' on critical literacy alerts us to the fact that there is not simply one, neat approach to critical literacy in primary classrooms, and the options open to us are many and varied. All of them, however, require us to engage with the premises and assumptions made about literacy, texts, social practice, and power that characterise each approach.

ACTIVITY 1

Analyse the 'definitions' of critical literacy provided below:

(a) Identify what they have in common, and what is different between them.

(b) Discuss or reflect on what this tells you about critical literacy and classroom practice.

Some 'definitions' of critical literacy

- 'Critical literacy, then, is learning to read and write as part of the process of becoming conscious of one's experience as historically constructed within specific power relations' (Anderson and Irvine 1993: 82).

- 'Critical reading is a stance—a strategy perhaps—which we can move in, one which usefully offers us a critical distance or a fresh perspective on what we would otherwise see as unworthy of comment. It makes the familiar strange' (Wallace 1992b: 12).

- For Ira Shor (1992: 32), critical literacy is 'analytic habits of thinking, reading, writing, speaking, or discussing which go beneath surface impressions, traditional myths, mere opinions, and routine clichés; understanding the social contexts and consequences of any subject matter; discovering the deep meaning of any event, text, technique, process, object, statement, image, or situation; applying that meaning to your own context.'

- 'It is through language that we come to an understanding of our world, and it is through language that our world is constructed. We therefore need to consider critically what and how we learn about our world (including ourselves) through reading, writing, and talking' (O'Brien 1994: 36).

- Chris Searle, writing about critical literacy: 'Working class children should learn to read, write, spell, punctuate, to develop the word as a weapon and tool in the inevitable struggles for improvement and liberation for them, and the rest of their class all over the world' (1993: 170).

- 'By "critical" we mean ways that give students tools for weighing and critiquing, analysing and appraising the textual techniques and ideologies, values and positions. The key challenge for teaching community texts, then, is how to engage students with study of "how texts work" semiotically and linguistically, while at the same time taking up explicitly how texts and their affiliated social institutions work politically to construct and position writers and readers in relations of power and knowledge (or lack thereof)' (Luke, Comber and O'Brien 1996: 35).

- 'In learning and using language, students are also learning cultural understandings and values. Therefore, they need to be able to reflect critically on what is being learned. The implication of this notion for teachers is that students need to be taught to recognise the social nature of the curriculum and other knowledge as well as to understand and construct alternative perspectives and informed personal meanings' (DECS 1996: 26).

- 'To use English appropriately, effectively and critically in a wide range of situations, students need to know the following:

    - That language is constructed, used and manipulated in powerful ways to influence others.

    - That because people interpret texts in the light of their own socio-cultural values and understandings, texts will have different meanings for different people. Students need to develop the ability to interpret texts . . . from perspectives other than their own' (Curriculum Corporation 1994: 10–11).

- 'Critical literacy depends on an understanding that language is a dynamic social process which responds to and reflects changing social conditions, and that the use of English is inextricably involved with values, beliefs and ways of thinking about ourselves and the world we inhabit. It involves an appreciation of and sensitivity to sociocultural diversity and an understanding that the meaning of any form of communication depends on context, purpose and audience' (CCWA 1998).

- 'Effective literacy teaching draws on knowledge and

understandings of the language resources which allow learners to . . . analyse texts critically, including asking the questions: "How is this text trying to influence me?" "If I am reading it, how is it positioning me with respect to the writer?" "If I am writing it, how am I positioning the reader with respect to me?"; and most generally, "What does this do to me?" '(NSWDSE 1997: 14).

- 'Critical literacy approaches are based on the belief that effective use of language requires people to explore the assumptions and the perspectives, both stated and unstated, on which texts are constructed . . . These approaches reject passive acceptance of texts at face value. Instead they require students to view a text from a variety of perspectives and to interpret various levels of meaning' (DEQ 1994: 2).

Some key assumptions

As noted in chapter 1, critical literacy is something of a chameleon, changing from context to context, and from one educational purpose to another. It has a number of aliases and emerges in different parts of the world as: critical language awareness, critical social literacy, critically-aware literacy, critical literacy awareness, and the like. From my reading and thinking about critical literacy, there are at least five elements or assumptions that characterise critical literacy approaches:

- Language education can make a real difference in students' lives, and particularly in the lives of students who fall outside the 'mainstream'.

- The meanings of words and texts construct, and are constructed by, cultural, social, historical, and political practices (that is, meanings are not 'natural' or 'neutral').

- Knowledge is not a fixed, objective body of ideas, but a social construction (eg what counts as 'knowledge' changes over time).

- Analysing and evaluating focuses on *something* for some *purpose*.

- Critical literacy includes some notion of what it means to be socially aware and active citizens. Teachers who subscribe to critical literacy have a stake in social change and aim at enabling students to investigate, question and challenge taken-as-natural relationships between language use and social practice.

All of these assumptions can be found in the different theoretical approaches to critical literacy (eg discourse, poststructuralist, feminist/masculinist, reader-response, functional grammar, Frierean approaches; see chapter 1).

Applying your understanding of critical literacy to classroom contexts

Sometimes it's easiest to begin with examining what critical literacy *isn't*. In my experience, teachers often claim they are 'doing' critical literacy, but oversimplify the relationships between language, power and social practice so that the activity merely becomes tricks with words.

An example of what NOT to do

This example is a 'virtual' one in that it isn't based on one single lesson I have observed; rather, it's an outcome of classroom observations, discussions with teachers and colleagues, and reading in the area.

A Year 4 teacher wanted to introduce his students to critical literacy by way of the notion that texts are always written from a particular 'point of view'. To do so, he first read them a traditional version of *The Three Little Pigs* (this was a 'sanitised' version where the wolf didn't get cooked and eaten by the third pig). As a class, they discussed the pictures in the book, focusing on the depiction of the Big Bad Wolf. Individually, each student then produced a 'wanted' poster for The Big Bad Wolf using a photocopied worksheet. The following day, the teacher read his students Jon Scieszka and Lane Smith's (1989) *The True Story of the 3 Little Pigs! By A. Wolf.* The students thoroughly enjoyed the tale, told by the wolf, of how he was framed by the media and was not the big, bad wolf he had been made out to be. The story was discussed and the main events summarised on the chalkboard in the form of a 'story map'. The class was then divided into small groups and given time to practise role playing either the traditional version of the three little pigs saga or the version told from the wolf's perspective (as allotted by their teacher). Later that week, the groups came together and watched each other's role play before discussing some of the differences between the two versions. The teacher then had students work in pairs to rewrite a number of other folktales from another character's point of view (eg the giant's perspective in *Jack and the Beanstalk*, Goldilocks' perspective in *Goldilocks and the Three Bears*). Later, when the texts were finished, the teacher introduced the term 'critical literacy' to the students and explained that that was what they had been doing for the past two weeks.

SOME QUESTIONS
- Given the perspectives and positions on critical literacy already discussed, what is it about this example that renders it 'a-critical' (ie not a critical literacy activity)?
- What literacy understandings does it actually develop/focus on?
- What theories of literacy and literacy learning appear to inform this activity?

The set of activities described above could be useful for developing notions of characters in texts, or for analysing authors' language choices. However, I do not consider this a sound approach to critical literacy as it oversimplifies the issue at stake (namely, that texts are never neutral, but are social constructions) by suggesting that 'author perspective' is simply a matter of character orientation. *There appears to be no real critique of why these texts were written, by whom, for what purposes, who was likely to read them (and who wasn't) and why, and what kind of view of the world was being promoted in and by these texts.*

To construct this kind of activity as a critical literacy one, a range of texts could be added and any or all of the following could be included:

- Examine folktales across time, from the original versions through to modern 'revisionist' tales and hypothesise about the role folktales play in our society, why versions have changed over, say, the last 200 years, and whether these changes have some connection to real life social changes (see, for example, Brack 1998).

- Use a series of critical text analysis questions developed by Gunther Kress and Cathie Wallace to 'interrogate' the author's worldview: values, beliefs, assumptions etc. (These questions are presented later in this chapter).

- Do away with literature altogether and use a real world event, such as a fight in the playground or other issues pertinent to students, and explore the different versions that get told as students describe what happened. This can then be extended to analysing—and critiquing—the way in which events are reported differently in different newspapers (eg local, state, national; across corporations) or on television across different channels (a commercial channel, SBS, and the ABC make for interesting comparisons). Government elections are also useful contexts for exploring worldviews and 'author position'. Other useful terrain includes the world of recipes (Where are they published? Who are they intended for? How do you know? Who would/wouldn't cook these things and why? Why have recipes for 'dieters' become more popular/available in the past 10 years? Who are they aimed at and why?) and travel blurbs (eg analysing descriptions of the same destination presented in, say, *Vogue*, *New Idea*, *The Australian*, and on the television show *The Great Outdoors* and relating this analysis to socioeconomic status, identity formation etc).

In thinking of these critical literacy activities I drew heavily on the '3D model' of literacy practice explained in the recent report, *Digital Rhetorics* (Lankshear et al 1998: 17), and based on earlier work by Bill Green (eg 1988; see also DECS 1996: 26). This 'model' or guiding framework develops a sociocultural view of literacy that has at least three interwoven dimensions: 'operational', 'cultural', and 'critical' (Green, 1997; Lankshear et al 1997, chapter 2). This takes into account language, meaning and context (Green 1988: 160–163; 1997).

Briefly, the *operational* dimension focuses on the *means* of literacy; that is, how people are, or become able to read and write *appropriately* in a range of contexts and for a range of purposes. In terms of literacy education, an operational focus deals to the technical or 'code-breaking' aspects of being 'literate'. The *cultural* dimension of the 3D model refers to the *meaning* aspect of literacy. This dimension of literacy recognises that language is not just a system (structured by rules etc), but a *system of meaning*. So, the cultural dimension of literacy is a matter of understanding texts in relation to contexts, which includes engaging with: the meaning of texts (including understanding their *content*); the meaning they need to make in order to be appropriate; and what it is about given contexts of practice that makes for appropriate or inappropriate ways of reading and writing.

Finally, the *critical* dimension refers to the *socially constructed* nature of all human practices and meaning systems. In order to be able to participate effectively and productively in any social practice, humans must be enculturated into it. But social practices and their meaning systems are always selective and represent particular interpretations and classifications of the ways in which the world 'works', or is believed to work by different groups of people. Unless individuals are also given access to the criteria used in selecting and the principles of interpretation they are merely enculturated or socialised into the meaning system (of a language/society) and unable to take an active part in its transformation; that is, they only have access to the cultural dimension of social practices and literacy. The critical dimension of literacy is the basis for ensuring that participants can only participate in a practice and make meanings within it, but can in various ways transform and actively produce it. An integrated approach to literacy education addresses all three dimensions simultaneously and equally.

Critical literacy and classrooms

ACTIVITY 2

This activity is drawn from Jennifer O'Brien's (eg 1994) work with Reception to Year 2 students. You will need to gather together a set of Mother's Day, Father's Day, Easter, or Christmas catalogues prior to this activity. Using the catalogues you've collected develop a literacy activity (for reading, writing, speaking and listening, or viewing) for a Year 1 or Year 2 class that *isn't* 'critical' in the sense we've been developing here and one that *is*.

For discussion

- How did you go about planning your critical literacy activity? What questions did you ask yourself? For example, 'How can I link this text to any social analysis or critique?' 'How can I get my students thinking about taken-for-granted assumptions operating in these advertising texts?' 'In what ways can I construct an activity that enables students to reflect on their own actions as consumers?' 'What social and cultural knowledge am I drawing on in constructing this activity?' 'What range of resources am I bringing to this activity in order to enhance it?'

- What aspects of the a-critical literacy activity 'changed' when you developed a critical literacy activity? Why?

- Write a short statement about what *you* think critical literacy is.

Remember that critical literacy is not about being simply negative. Rather, it means looking at something closely, analysing it, and then making a judgment or evaluation.

Critical literacy and text analysis

KEY QUESTIONS

What are the best pedagogical approaches to teaching critical literacy across all year levels, and what might be some of the problems that occur when implementing it in your classroom?

Despite the elusiveness of critical literacy theory, there are, thankfully, a number of strategies available to teachers for implementing critical literacy practices effectively in their classrooms. Many of these strategies tend to be text-based, and there are a number of premises about texts that are drawn from critical theory and that underpin these pedagogical approaches.

QUESTIONS

- What might some of these premises—or assumptions—about texts be? In other words, what kind of ***thing*** do you regard or know texts to be?

- What makes you think this? Or where does your knowledge and understanding of texts come from?

These premises include, in no particular order:

- All texts are ideological. There is no neutral position from which a text can be read, written, viewed, spoken etc.
- Texts (with some exceptions) are not deliberately or wickedly misleading.
- Texts do not mirror a single reality. Rather, texts construct particular versions of reality.
- There is no single, correct meaning of a text (although some 'readings' tend to be valued or accepted more than others in any given social group). Readings and writings are constructed in different social, historical, political and cultural contexts.
- Readers and writers generally construct meanings that support or affirm their particular value system and beliefs.

(Adapted from *Metropolitan East State School Support Centre* conference materials, Brisbane 1997.)

Pedagogical approaches to critical literacy include, among others:

- text analysis questions
- text clustering
- linguistic analysis of texts
- social semiotic analysis
- using historical information to critique social practices
- responding to social inequities and promoting social action by means of writing literary texts.

Text analysis questions

A number of educators interested in critical literacy have developed sets of analytical questions for interrogating the worldviews and assumptions that inform text construction (eg Wallace 1992a: 71; Kress 1985). The literacy focus of these questions is 'critical reading'.

SOME QUESTIONS FOR WORKING WITH YOUNGER READERS

- What is this text about? How do we know? Who would be most likely to read it and how do we know?
- What does the author want us to *know* (about the world and the people in it)? What do the pictures suggest? What do the words suggest? Does this 'match' what *you* know (about the world and about people)? Why/why not?

- What does the author want us to *believe* about the world and the people in it? What suggests this to us? Does this 'fit' with what *you* believe about the world and about people? Why/why not?

- How could we re-write this text so that it 'matches' more closely all of our experiences and fits more effectively with what we know about the world and about people?

(Note: These are very general questions, and it is expected that in a classroom context they are tailored explicitly to the text under study. For example, 'What claims are made about Weetbix on the packet? How do we know these claims are true? What effect do they have on you/us/someone who buys Weetbix?' Adapted from Comber and Simpson 1995).

SOME QUESTIONS FOR OLDER READERS

- What is the subject matter or topic?

- Why might the author might have written this text?

- Who is the intended audience? How do you know?

- What worldview and values does the author assume that reader holds? How do you know?

- What knowledge does the reader need to bring to this text in order to understand it?

- Who would feel 'left out' in this text, and why; and is it a problem? Who would find that the claims made in this text clash with their own values, beliefs or experiences?

- How is the reader 'positioned' in relation to the author (eg as a friend, as an opponent, as someone who needs to be persuaded, as invisible, as someone who agrees with the author's views)?

- Are there 'gaps' or 'absences' or 'silences' in this text? If so, what are they? For example, is there a group of people missing who logically should be included? Are different groups talked about as though they belong to the same, seamless group? Does the author write about a group without including *their* perspective on things or events?

ACTIVITY 3

Read the following advertising text taken from a mail order catalogue and then analyse it using the questions listed above.

'Sometimes in the thrill of the chase we forget the first rule of smart shopping. Just because something is cheap doesn't mean it's a great bargain. Before buying we should ask ourselves—Is it well made? Does it fit my lifestyle? Will it go with anything in my wardrobe? All these considerations add real value to every dollar we spend.

MONEY ISN'T EVERYTHING

For many of us, suits are a daily necessity, not a luxury. Value is a must. With this in mind, we've put together a fantastic range of interchangeable suit separates that feature classic, quality tailoring. A suit for under $140 definitely deserves a look, see pages 6 & 7. And when it comes to venturing outdoors you can't go past genuine shetland knits. We offer a choice of styles for both men and women. But good value isn't just restricted to the wardrobe. This month we feature a big section devoted to the home. Starting on page 54, we provide lots of ways to keep warm this winter without breaking the budget'

(from Myer Direct (1998) *Winter Values.* Melbourne: Myer Stores Ltd, p 2).

After analysing this text, consider the following:

- What do you 'discover' about this text when you 'unpack' it?

- What implications does this have for you as a consumer? As a teacher?

- Are there questions that could be added to the above list?

- What place might this kind of analysis have in, say, a Year 6 or a Year 7 class? And what responses could be generated out of this kind of analysis? (eg a letter to the company pointing out certain things and asking for them to be addressed).

Text clustering

This is simply a process of 'rubbing' different texts up against each other in order to, in Cathie Wallace's words, make the familiar strange. The theoretical focus of this pedagogical approach is to identify the ways in which texts 'construct' identities and/or subjectivies for different groups of people. By 'construct', we refer to the ways in which the language choices an author makes to describe or talk about a group of people—or an individual—aren't 'neutral' but are grounded in the author's view of the world, and in his or her values and beliefs, as well as in larger historical, social and political contexts and practices. Accordingly, how a group is written about—particularly if it is a marginal group being written about by someone who belongs to the 'mainstream' or dominant social group—isn't often how the group sees themselves or would choose to write about themselves.

ACTIVITY 4

- Jot down what you think 'being an Australian' means.

- Read the following texts and summarise the different 'constructions' of Australians operating in these texts.

FROM AN INTERACTIVE INTERNET SITE

I love all things Australian, is everyone in Australia as happy-go-lucky and friendly as Paul Hogan portrays? Anonymous.

> As a general Rule, yes—except for the people who aren't. It is probably important to note that not all Australians divorce their wives after 20-odd years of marriage and go off to America to marry young blondes and have absolutely no success at directing movies.

Every Australian I know (and I know quite a few) is funny, or at the very least, quite pleasantly amusing. Why is this? Bonni Hall, USA.

> Yes, it's true, Australians are funny. We are a naturally funny race. Because we live in a funny country, where people talk funny, have funny animals, drink funny beers, eat funny foods, and are generally a barrel of laughs all day.

We are having a fund-raising party with an Australian theme. What fabulous (and free or cheap) ideas can you give us to make it really fun? Anonymous.

> Well, I don't know about making it really fun, but here's a few ideas to give it an Australian theme:
>
> - Have a barbecue. For that authentic Australian suburban feel, cook snags (sausages) on it, put them in a slice of bread with some sauce (tomato ketchup) and/or bits of onion and charge a dollar each. Presto, instant Sausage Sizzle!
>
> - Get in some Vegemite, spread it thinly on toast and dare people to taste it.

(Source: *Toxic Custard Guide to Australia* http://www.toxiccustard.com/australia/culture.html Cited 5 June, 1998.)

FROM *HAPPY ISLES OF OCEANIA*

The Australian Book of Etiquette is a very slim volume, but its outrageous Book of Rudeness is a hefty tome. Being offensive, in a matey way, gets people's attention, and Down Under you often make friends by being intensely rude in the right tone of voice. Australian English (one of Australia's glories and its greatest artform) is a language of familiarity. *Goodoh! How yer doin' mate, all right? How's your belly where the pig bit yer?* Understanding the concept of mate ship is the key to success in Australia; and mockery is the assertive warmth of mateship (Theroux 1992: 23).

FROM A REVIEW OF BOOKS ABOUT AUSTRALIA

Italian writer Zaccaria Seriman, in 1749, published his spurious (as the Italian title would have translated) *Voyage of Henry Wanton to the Unknown South Land, and the Kingdom of Monkeys and Baboons*, in which the Antipodean inhabitants are illustrated as humans who dress in European clothes and live in houses but have the faces of monkeys and baboons. The book remained popular with several generations of readers (Turner 1998 23–24 May: 8).

> **QUESTIONS TO CONSIDER**
> - Which version of Australia/Australians is accurate? Why?
> - What other versions are available? From where?
> - What knowledge, understandings and experiences did you bring to your reading of the texts above?
> - How might you use texts like these in a classroom that includes ESL and NESB students?
> - List other possible clusters of texts you could use in your own classroom.

Linguistic analysis of texts

We can uncover the constructedness of texts in other ways, too. We can use functional grammar—or even traditional grammar for that matter—to home in on the *ideology* of a text (see especially Peter Wignell's chapter in this book). We define 'ideology' as a social theory or worldview that involves generalisations (beliefs, claims) about the ways in which the world 'works' (Gee 1996: 21). Therefore, we all subscribe to various ideologies that we use to make sense of our everyday lives.

ACTIVITY 5

Read the following then complete the tasks.

The Destruction of a Culture

Prior to the arrival of Europeans in Australia, the Aborigines lived orderly and socially stable lives based on values of co-operation and sharing. They had adapted and survived for at least 30,000 years in a continent with a diverse and harsh climate. This lifestyle changed with the arrival of the Europeans.

When different cultural groups who have different values and beliefs interact and meet, the smaller group often suffers from 'culture shock'. Its members become confused and bewildered about what is expected of them. This is what happened with the Aborigines. The European culture demanded certain things such as land-ownership, keeping domestic animals and private ownership which were in conflict with traditional Aboriginal beliefs. The Europeans had the military might and strength of numbers to support their viewpoint. (Hardie, Rutherford, and Walsh, 1987, p 58)

(Source: Luke and Freebody 1997: 205.)

- What genre is this text? How do you know?
- Who is it written for? How do you know? What knowledge did you draw on to answer this question?

Identify all of the human participants (nouns) and associated processes (verbs) in this excerpt. Draw up a table headed by these participants (eg Europeans/European culture, Aborigines/Aboriginal lifestyle) and list the processes under each appropriate heading.

- What you notice? (Use the text analysis questions from earlier in this chapter to inform your observations.)
- What implications does this analysis have for the kinds of texts you select for use in your classroom?
- Jot down ideas about ways of using this strategy with students in a range of year levels using data-base CD-ROM texts (eg Encarta, Groliers) or relevant websites.
- Reflect on ways in which skills-based and genre approaches can be made to work harmoniously (and theoretically coherently) with critical literacy.

KEY QUESTION
What are some of the texts and social practices children are likely to engage with in their everyday lives, and what impact—if any—should this have on the ways in which a teacher implements critical literacy in her or his classroom?

Whenever we 'do' critical literacy, it is important that we don't just confine ourselves to analyses of conventional texts. It is important to extend the reach of our analyses beyond texts to include analyses of social practices and to interrogate what are often 'taken-as-given' social practices and assumptions about the world.

Social semiotic analysis (a focus on 'viewing')

Investigating symbols and their social meanings can be a useful way of encouraging students to question where 'meanings' come from, and to see that *meaning* itself is a social construction rather than something inherent in words (and therefore separate from the messiness of everyday life). One way of making some cultural symbols more obvious is to videotape a music video clip that makes use of symbolism (eg Madonna's *Ray of Light*, 1998). Play the video a number of times to your students, then have them work on their own to jot down all the symbols they noticed. Beside each symbol, they are to write its (social) meaning (eg fast-motion clock hands—usually symbolises time rushing by). This may require a number of viewings (idea source: Michelle Brown and Kylie Newton, Albany State High School, ETAQ conference, 1996)

With my teacher education students, I have them compare their lists, and answer or do the following.

Questions to use with students

1 Why aren't your lists of symbols identical?

2 What knowledge, understandings or experiences did you draw on to give the meanings for the symbols?

3 Identify symbols that you have all written down, but have given different meanings to. Why has this happened?

4 How do 'symbols' come about?

Questions directed at professional development

1 For which year levels would this activity be most appropriate? Why?

2 What implications do your findings have for students and texts in general (you may want to focus on ESL students here)?

3 Design a follow-up activity for a designated year level.

If I was working with a class of primary school students, we may decide—as a result of discussing the first four questions above—to produce a 'guide to cultural symbols' that encompasses the different cultures we have access to in our class (this could include skateboard cultures, after-school-care cultures, ballet cultures, Scout cultures, etc). This draws directly on 'student as ethnographer' approaches pioneered by Shirley Brice Heath (eg 1983).

Using historical information

Often, constructions of and ways of thinking that we take for granted now are actually the result of historical forces and events. Critiquing a text is always enhanced by a complementary analysis of historical constructions of different groups of people.

ACTIVITY 6

Read and comment on the following. Consider some of the ramifications this kind of thinking has had over the centuries.

> Soon science itself was enlisted to the complementarian cause [a movement in the 1700s claiming men and women were different, but complementary] as practitioners in the emerging field of anatomy searched for scientific evidence of women's intellectual inferiority. After careful measurement, anatomists "discovered" that women's skulls were smaller in proportion to their bodies than men's. Thus, they said, the facts demonstrated that, as thinking beings, women were inferior to men. The problem with this deduction was that women's heads are actually larger in proportion to their bodies than men's. When anatomists were forced to concede this point in the nineteenth century, they did not thereby conclude that women had better brains; instead they interpreted the relatively larger head as a sign of incomplete growth. Cranial size was seen to indicate that women were closer to children, whose heads are also proportionately larger. Thus, again, women were construed as mentally inferior to men . . .

(Source: Margaret Wertheim (1996) *Pythagoras' Trousers*. London: Fourth Estate, p 148.)

The social construction of gender is not the only construction occurring in our society. For example, there is a popular myth that suggests children from working-class homes do not have regular access to a range of texts, or that their parents just aren't interested in—or value—education. This sets up particular constructions of working-class students as having a 'deficit' or different values so that school failure becomes their fault alone, and not a problem of schooling or education in general.

- Identify other kinds of social constructions and identify possible 'popular myths' that are used to promote these constructions, and who might consciously or unconsciously subscribe to these myths as 'truth'.

- Design ways of showing these 'assumptions' to be 'myths' in a classroom context (books on urban myths prove invaluable here).

Responding to social inequities

Chris Searle (eg 1993, 1998) has developed an approach to critical literacy that uses poetry (and other literary and information texts) to explore—and imaginatively empathise with the people involved in—real-life issues from multiple perspectives (eg wars in the Arab Gulf, Bosnia and the Falklands; racism; poverty). He works with low socioeconomic students in extremely multicultural schools—with groups of students who are traditional cultural enemies, with students who have been 'written off' by other schools, and students who are alienated from school and life in general. His approach to critical literacy is outlined in chapter 7 in this collection.

ACTIVITY 7

Read the following contextual notes and poem (from Searle 1998: 135).

The students were working with imaginative empathy to imagine themselves into the lives and feelings of people in troubled places around the world (eg Soweto, Hebron, Kashmir). In her poem one Pakistani girl 'expressed the determination of an elderly South African woman voting for the first time in a meaningful election' despite intimidation and the very real danger of death:

I WASN'T SCARED

I was walking with my grandchildren,
A bomb exploded right behind me.
I didn't run
I wasn't scared
I walked ahead
Knowing I was going to get to the polling station.
Before my death
I will vote!

Shaista

TASK

Identify the kinds of teaching and learning practices most likely to have occurred in Shaista's classroom in order for her to produce such an evocative and meaningful poem.

Consider the resources her teacher might have used, the kind of 'contextualising' knowledge and understanding the students would need before beginning to write, the kind of modelling and scaffolding that might have occurred in terms of writing poems, what kinds of learning management strategies—eg small group work, pair work, editors' circles, readers' theatre—might be most effective etc.

Critical perspectives on teaching practice

KEY POINT
Becoming an effective critical literacy educator requires you to develop 'metalevel' perspectives on literacy **per se**, as well as on your literacy teaching practices and the literacy experiences you make available to your students.

> **QUESTIONS**
> - What does this mean, and do you agree? Why/why not?
> - What implications does this statement hold for classroom practice?

Critical literacy is more than just doing things with texts. It is a perspective or way of looking at things. This includes looking at our own personal ideologies and the impact they have on our literacy teaching. This encompasses the literacy resources we use and bring into our classroom (both professional and resource texts), the ways in which we construct what 'counts' as literacy in our class (eg whether or not we see video game reviews as legitimate texts to read or write in school and why), and even the ways in which we speak to our students and manage our class.

Whose cultural knowledge 'counts'

Even something as seemingly simple as a traditional reading comprehension test is far from neutral. For example, answer the following questions without reading the text that originally accompanied them in the *SRA Reading Laboratory* kit (Parker c1959) from which it was taken.

HOW WELL DID YOU READ?

What happened in the story?

1. Danny's mother said that Skip had to
    - A. learn to obey
    - B. stay out of the house
    - C. live somewhere else

2. The instructor told Danny that
    - A. Skip should come to school alone
    - B. Danny's mother should attend school
    - C. both Skip and Danny should attend

3. The instructor told the class that the dogs would learn
    - A. to obey four important commands
    - B. to do tricks
    - C. to jump on strangers

Did you understand?

4. When a dog heels, he walks

    A. in front of his master

    B. behind his master

    C. beside his master

5. When a dog obeys, you should

    A. not say anything

    B. scold him

    C. praise him

6. 'Come' is an important command because it can

    A. make a dog walk beside you

    B. call a dog away from danger

    C. keep a dog from jumping on people

ACTIVITY 8

- What knowledge did you draw on to answer these questions?

- Which questions gave you trouble? Why/Why not?

- So, what is this kind of comprehension test testing when we stop to think about it?

- What implications does this have for assumptions we make about our students and their literacy abilities?

- What implications does this have for the texts and tests we elect to use in our classroom?

- Those interested in the cultural dimensions of knowledge might like to follow up Pierre Bourdieu's (1986) work on 'cultural capital'.

What literacy practices are excluded

Critical literacy and genre theory can fit together logically and coherently (both come under the umbrella of 'sociocultural literacy theories'), as we saw earlier in this chapter. Critical literacy insights can also be used to *inform the ways in which teachers teach genres*—however, this aspect is often overlooked, as demonstrated by Barbara Kamler:

> While the work on genre has been important in providing useful critiques of process pedagogy and in calling attention to the larger dis-

course structures of text, there are enormous difficulties with the genre based work, in particular the formulaic implementation, its narrow focus on language and text and its lack of attention to the institutional and disciplinary contexts in which texts are constructed. To illustrate I will use a brief example of a misogynist text written in a classroom where genre based pedagogy was implemented. The text is called *Girls into Concrete*.

Girls into concreate [sic]
This potion will turn girls into concreate

Ingrediance

1 kg of concreate

2 girls

1 eye from a bat

Method

1. tip 1 kg of concreate into tub

2. drop eye into concreate in tub

3. put girls into concreate. Make sure that girls are sitting up right

Note

This potion will not work if add too much concreate

Kamler discusses how a teacher used this text she had collected from her classroom to analyse—using functional grammar and genre theory—for an assignment in a graduate diploma class Kamler was teaching. The teacher commented on the structure of the procedural text, the use of material processes in the imperative mood, sequencing, authoritative and impersonal tenor, and the like. She concluded her analysis with 'While I would classify [this text] as a complete instructional procedural genre, it would have been even better with a concluding step after step 3 of the method – eg, 4) When concrete girls have set they can be used as ornaments in home or garden.' (Kamler 1996: 10).

ACTIVITY 9

- What do you make of the teacher's assessment of this text? (ie What's going on here?)

- Using what you now know about critical literacy, critically analyse the recipe text. What would be your feedback to (a) the student who composed this text and (b) your advice to the teacher who only analysed the generic features of the text?

Constructing versions of literacy

This is addressed more directly in the following chapter by Colin Lankshear, but for any critical literacy practitioner it is important to reflect on one's own language, literacy and social practices connected with teaching. For example, a teacher who spends time in class analysing and critiquing gender roles in picture book narratives, then insists on separate lines for boys and girls, or who differentiates classroom tasks along gender lines (eg girls water the plants while boys empty the bin) is sending out mixed messages to students.

If you are interested in following up on the relationships between classroom discourses and classroom literacy practices, the following are 'must reads': James Paul Gee (eg 1996), Shirley Brice Heath (1983), Carolyn Baker and Peter Freebody (1989), and Courtney Cazden (1988).

Conclusion

To sum up, it seems to me that in order to practise critical literacy effectively in primary classrooms, teachers need to have a *social theory* as well as a theory of literacy. That is, they need to have some notion of how things 'operate' in the world, and how some of these things advantage certain groups of people over others. In addition, teachers need access to a rich repertoire of teaching strategies that promote *active* learning in their classrooms. This includes strategies for:

- Scaffolding students' questioning techniques so that they become proficient at constructing and employing effective questions for a range of information-gathering and analytic purposes.

- Developing students' abilities to 'research' a topic or issue that goes beyond simply having them use two information texts to produce a 'project' on a country or product. This includes teaching students how to operate an array of information sources and resources, how to construct logical and coherent arguments, how to evaluate and synthesise information from a number of different sources, how to evaluate claims made in speeches, television news reports, newspapers etc.

- Modelling strategies—and allowing spaces for students to practise them—that are used in critiquing claims and assumptions that appear to underpin texts, social practices etc. This includes, for example, showing students how to compare and contrast claims or facts, how to problematise 'facts', how to question the assumptions and worldviews underwriting a text or social practice.

- Providing students with a range of dynamic learning contexts that range across different groupings (eg individual, small group, whole class) and sites (eg classroom, local shopping centre, parks).

In a critical literacy approach, each activity and its accompanying texts require consideration of the social practices, histories, and other forces coordinating and producing various 'readings' of reality. The activities offered in this chapter are starting points only, and will simply become 'tricks with texts' if lifted straight from the page.

References

Anderson, G and Irvine, P (1993) 'Informing critical literacy with ethnography', in C Lankshear & P McLaren (eds), *Critical Literacy: Politics, Praxis, and the Postmodern*. State University of New York, Albany, pp 81–104.

Baker, C and Freebody, P (1989) *Children's First School Books*. Oxford: Basil Blackwell.

Bourdieu, P (1986) *Distinction: A Social Critique of the Judgement of Taste*. Trans. R. Nice. London: Routledge.

Brack, C (1998) 'Fairy stories and critical literacy', in D Bradshaw (ed) *Knowledge of texts: Theory and Practice in Critical Literacy*. Melbourne: Language Australia, pp 45–68.

Cazden C (1988) *Classroom Discourse*. Portsmouth, New Hampshire: Heinemann.

Comber, B and Simpson, A (1995) 'Reading cereal boxes: Analysing everyday texts', in P Adams and H Campagna-Wildash (compilers) *texts: The Heart of the English Curriculum*. No 1. Adelaide: DECS.

Curriculum Corporation (1994) *A Statement on English for Australian Schools*. Carlton, Victoria: Curriculum Corporation.

CCWA (Curriculum Council Western Australia) (1998) *Curriculum Framework for the English Learning Area (Kindergarten to Year 12)*. Perth: Curriculum Council.

DEQ (Department of Education, Queensland) (1994a) *A Guide to Using English Syllabus Materials*. Brisbane: Department of Education.

DECS (Department for Education and Children's Services, SA) (1996) *Literacy and Statements and Profiles: An Introduction to Addressing Literacy in Areas of Study*. Adelaide: Department for Education and Children's Services.

NSWDSE (New South Wales Department of School Education) (1997) *Focus on Literacy: A Position Paper on the Teaching of Literacy*. Sydney: NSWDSE Curriculum Directorate.

Freebody, P (1992) 'A socio-cultural approach: Resourcing four roles as a literacy learner', in A Watson and A Badenhop (eds) *Prevention of Reading Failure*. Sydney: Ashton Scholastic, pp 48–60.

Freebody, P and Luke, A (1990) 'Literacies programs: Debates and demands in cultural context'. *Prospect*. Vol 5, No 7, pp 7–16.

Gee, J (1996) *Social Linguistics and Literacies: Ideology in Discourses*. London: Falmer Press.

Gilbert, P (1993) '(Sub)versions: Using sexist language practices to explore critical literacy'. *Australian Journal of Language and Literacy*. Vol 16, No 4, pp 323–332.

Green, B (1997) 'Literacy, information and the learning society'. Keynote address at the Joint Conference of the Australian Association for the Teaching of English, the Australian Literacy Educators' Association, and the Australian School Library Association. Darwin: Darwin High School, Northern Territory, Australia, 8–11 July.

Green, B (1988) 'Subject-specific literacy and school learning: A focus on writing'. *Australian Journal of Education*. Vol 32, No 2.

Heath, S (1983) *Ways With Words: Language, Life and Work in Community and Classrooms*. Cambridge: Cambridge University Press.

Kamler, B (1995) 'The grammar wars'. *English in Australia*. No 114, pp 3–15.

Kress, G (1985) *Linguistic Processes in Sociocultural Practice*. Geelong: Deakin University Press.

Lankshear, C and Bigum, C et al (1997) *Digital Rhetorics: Literacies and Technologies in Education: Current Practices and Future Directions*. Vols 1–3. Project Report. Children's Literacy National Projects. Brisbane: QUT/DEETYA.

Luke, A, Comber, B and O'Brien, J (1996) 'Critical literacies and cultural studies', in G Bull and M Anstey (eds) *The Literacy Lexicon*. Sydney: Prentice Hall, pp 31–46.

Luke, A and Freebody, P (1997) 'Shaping the social practices of reading', in S Muspratt, A Luke, P Freebody (eds) *Constructing Critical Literacies: Teaching and Learning Textual Practice*. Sydney: Allen and Unwin, pp 185–225.

O'Brien, J (1994) 'Critical literacy in an early childhood classroom: A progress report'. *Australian Journal of Language and Literacy Education*. Vol 17, No 1, pp 36–44.

Parker, D (c1959) *SRA Reading Laboratory*. Chicago: Science Research Associates.

Scieszka, J and Smith, L (1989) *The True Story of the 3 Little Pigs! By A. Wolf*. London: Puffin.

Searle, C (1993) 'Words to a life-land: Literacy, the imagination, and Palestine', in C Lankshear and P McLaren (eds) *Critical Literacy: Politics, Praxis, and the Postmodern*. Albany, New York: State University of New York.

Searle, C (1998) *None But Our Words*. Buckingham, UK: Open University Press.

Shor, I (1992) *Empowering Education: Critical Teaching for Social Change*. Chicago: University of Chicago Press.

Theroux, P. (1992) *Happy Isles of Oceania*. London: Hamish Hamilton.

Turner, B. (1998) 'Terrible Australis', *Weekend Australian Review*, 23–24 May: p 8.

Wallace, C (1992a) *Reading*. Oxford: Oxford University Press.

Wallace, C (1992b) 'Critical literacy awareness in the EFL classroom', in N Fairclough (ed) *Critical Language Awareness*. London: Longman.

CHAPTER 9

Literacy and critical reflection

COLIN LANKSHEAR

In this chapter, Colin Lankshear highlights the importance of developing a critically reflective approach to literacy teaching. He proposes that effective critical literacy pedagogy includes teachers examining closely their own values, beliefs and world views and the ways in which these impinge on their teaching practices. Lankshear uses one student's literacy experiences at school and at home to illustrate the importance of reflecting critically on classroom constructions of literacy education. He wraps up with a discussion of the often tenuous relationship between the literacies practised in classrooms and authentic literacy practices in the 'real world'.

The previous chapters in this book have explored various approaches to critical literacy. They have addressed different areas and themes for doing critical literacy work. And they have considered how critical literacy might be built into classroom language programs. This chapter will consider the importance of reflecting critically on our beliefs, assumptions, theories and practices as teachers concerned with literacy education.

As we saw in chapter 1, reflecting critically on literacy does not necessarily involve taking a *negative* stance toward what we are reflecting on. Rather, it means looking at something closely, analysing it and then making a judgment or evaluation. In some cases this judgment or reflection *might* suggest (negatively) a need for change or improvement. On the other hand, however, it might equally well be affirming or positive. The point about including a critical perspective in our approach to work and in other important dimensions of our lives is to 'keep an eye on things', and not become complacent, take things for granted or operate on false or inadequate assumptions. Being 'critical' in this sense is about trying to do and be the best that we can. To use some contemporary jargon, it is about a serious search for 'continuous improvement'.

Critical reflection always requires some kind of standpoint or 'values orientation'. It involves more than just having a set of techniques, methods or skills for reflecting and evaluating. Whenever we reflect critically on something, we do so in the light of some goals or ideals or criteria; in the light of some standards, purposes, or values that we believe are appropriate.

For example, let's assume we are committed to 'inclusive education' as an important value or ideal for teaching and learning. In this case, to reflect critically on our practice as literacy educators would involve, among other things, examining and evaluating our practice in terms of its *inclusiveness*. In our critical reflection we would ask such things as whether what we did in class excluded anyone and, if so, who? How did it exclude them, and could this be avoided? Is our concern to be inclusive in tune with other goals and values, or are we giving it too much or too little attention? Have we got the right balance between, say, being inclusive and being *effective* in getting our overall goals achieved?

This example shows us something else besides the fact that critical reflection involves a values standpoint as well as techniques or skills of critique. It suggests also that our critical reflection must from time to time be about our *values and goals*—our 'standpoint'—as well as about more concrete and immediate things like our programs and pedagogy. It may involve reflecting critically on particular goals or values *in their own right*, or it may be a matter of critiquing the *relative weight* we give to our goals and our priorities: am I giving too much attention to being inclusive, and not enough to promoting excellence? If so, is this a problem of my *priorities* or *emphasis* among my goals and values? Are my priorities okay, and the problem simply that I need to improve my methods for promoting excellence, or for catering to the needs of 'high fliers'? And so on. As we will see a little later, one of the things we may have to reflect upon critically is our understanding of literacy itself.

In this chapter I draw on a 'real life' example to provide a *context* for critical reflection on things to do with literacy teaching and learning. This is the example of Jacques, a real student from a real classroom. Jacques is an example of what is called a 'telling case'. He is not your 'average', 'typical' or 'normal' student—he is not representative of learners at large. But neither is he atypical. We all have known many students like Jacques. Rather, Jacques provides an excellent example of one kind of 'benchmark' against which we might analyse and evaluate different aspects of classroom-based literacy education. Many other kinds of benchmarks exist, but Jacques will serve very well for looking at this question of critical reflection.

Jacques: A telling case

The student

At the time of the study on which this case is based (Knobel 1997, 1998), Jacques was 13 years old and in Year 7. He was a likable popular lad, with a keen sense of humour which used complex intertextual language patterns. Jacques could parody situations, conversations, and people with ease. His oral language was skilled and highly tuned, a quality noted by his teacher.

In class, however, Jacques was easily distracted and often quickly lost track of the learning activities and purposes in process around him. He would maintain a steady 'patter' of commentary—humorous asides, chatter, banter—on what was happening as it was happening. He rarely contributed, or was invited to contribute, in any substantial way to lesson events.

Jacques had repeated Year 1, and was described by his current teacher as 'having great difficulty with literacy'. He had little success making connections between what the teacher was trying to make explicit about literacy skills, processes and meta-cognitive strategies, and the tasks the class was subsequently engaged in.

Snapshot 1: Compare and contrast activity

(Monday 14 November 1994, Day 7 of observations)

EVENT: LANGUAGE LESSON
SUBEVENT 1: READING INFORMATION SHEET (PAIR WORK)
(9:47 am) Ms Bryant tells students to take out their language books and explains, 'You'll be working in pairs today.' She hands out a photocopied information sheet on Balinese customs to the students, along with an Open Compare and Contrast proforma. Ms Bryant tells students to take turns reading. Sean starts reading and Jacques mutters to me, 'I hate reading. It's boring.' Sean keeps reading and Jacques comments, 'Boring, hey'. 'You're not wrong', replies Sean. 'C'mon. Keep going', counters Jacques, and then pretends to fall into a deep sleep. They discuss Sean's recent trip 'down the coast', and Jacques talks about accidentally knocking over a girl at rollerskating.

SUBEVENT 2: LEARNING TASK (WHOLE CLASS)
(9:50 am) Jacques and Sean have read only three paragraphs when Ms Bryant brings the class together again. She explains again, 'I want you to use this sheet,' holding up a copy of the proforma they have in front of them, 'to compare and contrast Balinese and Australian customs. You have to identify what is the same and what is different between them, and write them in the appropriate spaces'. Ms Bryant reprimands Jacques for pretending to give Sean electric shocks. She then asks various children to read aloud consecutive paragraphs. After each paragraph, she identifies things in common to both cultures, and discusses some of their differences. For example, she points out that 'Both cultures have ceremonies to mark special times in your life, like birthdays and anniversaries.' Sean and others begin writing while Ms Bryant is speaking, and she reminds the class, 'It'd be good if not just one of the partners did all the writing'. Sean throws down his pen and tells Jacques to finish the word.

After a short while, Ms Bryant interrupts the class, asking 'Who knows what placenta is?' in response to a student's question and prompted by the text he was reading. When no-one offers an explanation, Ms Bryant briefly describes what it is and its function.

Jacques and Sean share a running meta(con)textual commentary on proceedings (eg Ms Bryant talks about baptism and Jacques declares softly: 'Yeah, and Sean was dropped'.) Ms Bryant directs the class to complete the compare and contrast proforma, using information from the sheet and what they know about Australia.

SUBEVENT 3: WORK TASK (PAIR WORK)

A student asks Ms Bryant what they're supposed to write, and she replies, 'I've already told the class twice', then moves off to help another student. Jacques turns to Sean and asks with a wide yawn: 'What have we gotta write? She didn't even say.' Sean doesn't seem to know and they ask Nikki, who tells them to write something about baptism. Jacques asks Ms Bryant to clarify the task, claiming he couldn't hear what she was saying. Ms Bryant explains again.

(10:15 a.m) Sean works on the proforma while Jacques sits and yawns, looks around, or fiddles with a pencil.

In this lesson, as in all the others observed, the teacher carefully demonstrated, explained and scaffolded the meta-cognitive strategies she was trying to teach the class, and referred to them frequently. For example, the students have just finished reading a short, photocopied text titled *What is race?*, and have been asked to identify key words in the article. After walking around checking students' work, Ms Bryant asks the class: 'Do you think that "moved apart" is a key word? Remember I said to you that key words are like if you saw them on their own, you'd be pretty much able to tell what the whole text is talking about. If I said "colour, ethnic background, human species, ancestry, groups", could you sort of tell what I was talking about?' The students answer 'Yes', and Ms Bryant then provides scaffolds for their understanding by working methodically through the text, helping different students to identify key words.

Later, Ms Bryant revisited the persuasive exposition (argument) text type with her students:

'We're going to try an write an argument about racial stereotypes. Remember the one we read about skateboarding? We talked about the special format [indicates model and proforma they had glued into their workbooks]. Their topic was "Skateboard riding is not an acceptable school activity". And we read arguments "for" or "against" it.' She briefly reminded students of the arguments used by the writers to construct the different positions. 'Right, so the first things you need is an "opening comment"'. As a class they review the opening comment of one of the 'skateboarding' texts. 'So what do I mean when I say "Write an opening comment?"' . . . 'An opening comment tells whether the writer agrees with the topic, or doesn't. Then you have to give your viewpoint or argument—sometimes called a "thesis".' Together, they worked through the generic features of an 'argument', used samples provided and written by Ms Bryant as models. Ms Bryant actively modelled an argument for the students, using the *What is Race?* text as a springboard. She talked her arguments through for the students, explained how to 'develop an argument' and listed words on the chalkboard that she thought she might need (eg recognise, must, to use, have to). She then asked students to draft or 'write a preview' of their own arguments against racism. The lesson continued with Ms Bryant monitoring students' work and providing feedback or input wherever needed.

In spite of the teacher's careful explanations, modelling and demonstrations, Jacques seemed often not to understand the purpose of the strategies or 'templates'—such as the compare and contrast proforma, or the one used to guide their expository argument writing. For instance, immediately after the lesson session described above, students went to work on their projects. One task involved doing an 'open compare and contrast' on countries. When Jacques asked the teacher 'What's a compare and contrast?', he seemed genuinely surprised when she glared at him and walked away.

Jacques had a straightforward perception of himself as a learner. 'I'm like my Dad, I'm not a pencil man.' 'I'm not keen on language and that.' 'I hate reading.' In class he certainly seemed disengaged from most academic-type activities. At his desk he would break up time with regular yawns, heavy sighs, fidgeting with pens and water bottles, feigning sleep with head on desk, and shifting restlessly in his seat. Unless constantly supervised, he completed very little schoolwork, and had developed an entire repertoire of work avoidance and resistance strategies: looking for items he had apparently misplaced, delegating tasks to others, 'helping' others instead of working (eg filling glue pots), claiming he hadn't heard instructions, and spending time planning what to do (Knobel 1997: 223).

One of his more celebrated literacy 'accomplishments' in class took the form of a sophisticated lampooning of process writing, and the 'writing centre' which the teacher had set up in a corner of the room to display various ways of publishing stories. During the first term when the class did 'general process writing', Jacques spent his time at the 'centre' over two days cutting out and stapling two tiny booklets about 6 cm by 4 cm, each containing several pages. In these he wrote two or three words per page over a one- or two-week period to produce 'narratives' of around 10–15 words. His peers found these hilarious when Jacques read them to different groups during breaks in lessons (he produced six 'J P Stories' in all). The teacher saw this as Jacques avoiding writing—'his spelling is poor, so he doesn't like to write'—and turning his writing into a joke so as not to take it too seriously or get too bothered about it. She described the stories as 'very, very childish', albeit highly amusing to the class.

The literate worker–entrepreneur

This sketch of Jacques' 'classroom literacy life' contrasts starkly with his out-of-school experiences. He is adept with machinery, enjoys working at every opportunity with his father in the family's earthmoving business, and looks forward to leaving school in Year 10 and going to work. He 'learned' to drive at 7 years of age, when his father asked him on the job

```
                    J.P.s
            MOWING        SERVICE

           -- Efficient, reliable service.

           -- Grass clippings removed.

           -- All edging done.

           -- First time lawn cut FREE!
                ( only regular customers )

           -- For free quote Ph 263 5594
```

FIGURE 9.1: Jacques' flier (A4)

one day to move a vehicle—which Jacques promptly did. These days, during his holidays, Jacques operates heavy vehicles under supervision and, in his Dad's words, 'works harder than a lot of 20-year-olds I know'. When Jacques spoke of what learning means to him and its significance, he always related it to being able to perform well as a worker. 'If you want to put gravel on a road you need to know how many square metres you need.' He saw 'being a dud' (learning failure) in terms of not being able to apply learning in practical contexts like work.

His immersion in a business culture at home and his orientation toward work are apparent in examples like the following. Prior to his summer holidays, and with some assistance from his mother and brother, Jacques produced on his father's computer a flier to launch and advertise 'JP's Mowing Service'.

Having posted the flier in local letterboxes, Jacques soon had a profitable weekend and holiday enterprise. Speaking about the language he used in the flier, Jacques explained he had included 'First time lawn cut free' to entice customers. 'So they'll all go, "Oh yeah, this is great" (miming a double take) Whhhttt!! (grabs the flier) "What's that number again?!"' (mimes dialling frantically). The smaller font for 'Only regular customers' likewise imitates commercial fliers, suggesting Jacques' meta-level understanding of how literacy operates in business discourse.

The literate witness

The contrast between the literacy of 'J P's Mowing Service' and that of Jacques' classroom life could hardly be more extreme. Similar contrasts are evident in aspects of his out-of-school literacy associated with being a Jehovah's Witness. For example, the family attends Theocratic School each week, where Jacques is regularly required to read and explain biblical texts to assemblies of up to 100 people. These reading, speaking and exegetic performances are scrutinised and evaluated publicly by members of the assembly, who use official criteria and checklists taken from Theocratic School literature. To prepare for his presentations Jacques works with his mother. Together they write the introductions and conclusions. His mother explicitly provides scaffolds for Jacques' learning and (subsequent) fluent performance by reading the text onto a tape for Jacques to follow as he rehearses reading the text aloud.

On Saturdays Jacques does door-to-door witnessing, dressed in suit, shirt and tie, and carrying his briefcase. He needs to be familiar with the literature they show, and be able to discuss personal values, religious beliefs and social issues with diverse kinds of people. While Jacques sometimes participated reluctantly in the literacy practices associated with his faith, the amount and the quality of public and private reading, speaking, and writing he does around his affiliation as a Jehovah's Witness, and his application to these practices, far outweigh his engagement in literacy work at school.

So what?

It's not easy to get data like this on our students—let alone on *all* of them. But it's worth remembering that when we hear talk about 'teachers as researchers' it is getting this kind of picture and perspective that is often the most valuable kind of research outcome. All too often I hear about 'teacher–researchers' who want to launch 'action research projects' on their schools, students and communities, without first having any clear sense of *who* these people are, what *they* know, what can be learned from *them*, or even what kind of data is most useful to obtain and what to do with it when it is obtained. Indeed, it is not even necessary that we gather data *ourselves* to help us reflect upon and better understand matters of literacy and pedagogy. Many excellent resources are *already* available that we can use to spark our own critical reflection (eg Gee 1996; Heath 1982, 1983; Hill et al 1998; Knobel 1998; Michaels 1981, 1985; Yeager, Floriani and Green 1998). They will also inform us usefully about what kinds of data we might usefully gather, how to gather it sensitively, ethically and effectively, how to use it once we've got it, and so on. Of course, it is unrealistic to expect teachers to research the in-school and out-of-school lives of every student in their classes to the extent that Jacques has been. This is what makes the research described in resources like those identified above all the more useful to time-pressed classroom teachers. In research by Susan Hill et al (1998) are examples of teachers who are aware of the lives of students beyond the classroom and the 'funds of knowledge' they bring with them to school-based learning.

To return to the example at hand, how might 'telling cases' like Jacques stimulate critical reflection on the part of literacy teachers? What makes Jacques a 'telling case'? What kinds of 'rethinkings' can such cases stimulate? What sorts of issues might they generate for us to be alert to, and try to address, in our programming, planning and practice?

In the final section I consider some of the possibilities for critical reflection that arise from the example of Jacques. Hopefully, this will help to encourage critical reflection about literacy and pedagogy on the part of readers, as well as provide some 'scaffolding' and 'models' for such reflection.

Critical reflection on literacy in theory and practice: Starting from Jacques

What are some of the things cases like that of Jacques might challenge us to reflect upon critically: that is, to re-examine closely, analyse, evaluate and, where appropriate, revise? I see at least four points worth considering here.

Our understanding of literacy

Traditionally, the dominant 'take' on literacy among educators has been one of cognitive skills and processes involved in reading and writing, of decoding and encoding print. Making learners literate has been seen in terms of getting eye, hand, and brain 'in sync' in such ways as identifying letters, relating letters and sounds, combining sounds and letters, forming words, tracking words across a page, and 'getting' or 'communicating' meanings via the words in a text. According to this view, once people have mastered such basic skills and processes they can then use them in all sorts of contexts and activities, and go on with learning many other things.

From this viewpoint, a lot of the key questions about teaching literacy concern what are the best print *resources* to use in teaching these skills (eg what *kind* of basal readers?; what *kind* of word lists?, and what kinds of *techniques* and *approaches* work most effectively (eg. phonics, look and say, whole language). So far as the matter of a *context* for literacy learning is concerned, it is seen as the classroom setting of teacher, learner, print resources, teacher aide etc. The skills and processes of reading and writing are themselves seen as 'universal' and 'self-contained'. They are seen as independent of context, existing in their 'own right', and being essentially the same always and everywhere they are used.

Recently, this view has been seriously challenged by a 'sociocultural' view of literacy. This denies the idea that literacy can be reduced to skills and processes of decoding and encoding, which can then be *generalised* to all sorts of contexts. Instead, the sociocultural view says we can only understand reading and writing within the contexts of the particular social and cultural practices in which they occur in concrete instances.

This is based on the idea that to 'read or write something', in any serious sense of the term, is to read or write it with *understanding*—in this sense, I cannot read chemistry books. This understanding *always* involves more than just what is in the code. Different kinds of texts require different kinds of learning backgrounds and different kinds of understandings and skills if they are to be read or written *meaningfully*. This is why, for example, a Christian fundamentalist and a liberation theologist might read the same biblical texts in radically different ways—making very different meanings. The two can be said to be reading the same set of words out of very different social practices: with different assumptions, underlying beliefs, purposes, values, ideological commitments and so on. So far as these two literacies are concerned, what is interesting about them and the differences between them actually has very little to do with the 'skills and processes' so often equated with *literacy* (for further development of these ideas, see Gee, Hull and Lankshear 1996: 1–4).

Learning how to read and write particular texts meaningfully involves taking part in social practices where these texts are read in a certain kind of way; and talked about in a certain kind of way; and where participants hold certain kinds of attitudes and values in relation to these texts; and interact around them in certain ways (Gee, Hull and Lankshear 1996: 3). To refer back to Jacques, we can see how his 'Theocratic School literacy' and his 'business flier literacy' reflect his participation in particular kinds of practices, with distinctive kinds of values, purposes, assumptions, underlying beliefs, kinds of interaction, rules for getting it right and wrong, and so on. Once again, the serious learning that has to go on for mastery of these literacies involves much more than just the 'skills and processes' of encoding and decoding. Handling these literacies to the point where they are meaningful involves a vast amount of learning that has little or nothing to do with the 'text skills stuff', and a lot to do with the wider practice in which the texts and the literacy are embedded.

In Jacques' case, we can see that the texts he encounters and produces in his 'business' and 'church' contexts of practice are indeed *meaningful* to him. They are meaningful to him at two levels. First, he understands the meaning of these texts in the sense of 'what they say'. But they are also meaningful to him in the larger sense that he understands 'where they are at', or what the practice is that these texts belong to are 'on about' in the first place. He understands what it *means* to participate in Theocratic School, or to be involved in trying to drum up business by producing a flier.

As a result, when he is asked about the literacies involved in these practices he is able to give clear answers that reflect genuine understanding. At home, for instance, he engaged in 'compare and contrast' exercises often, when deciding which of two things would make the better purchase. Of course, he did not *call* this 'comparing and contrasting'. But he knew what he was doing and why, and could explain his decisions clearly and well. In these domains his language and literacy activity was highly meaningful and, correspondingly, effective and successful.

This, however, was very obviously *not* the case in a lot of his school literacy. In many cases he didn't get the point of *that* at all. And with the help of a sociocultural view of literacy we can begin to see why. The literacy practices he 'reads out of' in his home and community life—his primary *meaningful* life—are very different from his school literacy practices. The former have quite distinctive purposes and routines which he has grown up immersed in; which he understands; and which for him provide 'blueprints' for meaningful text-related practices. Making the link to characteristically 'school-like' literacies—like process story writing in the writers' centre—is difficult. After all, these school practices must seem awfully odd to someone coming from Jacques' kind of contexts. How *would* the handler of heavy machinery with his head in the space of cubic metres of gravel per job, and first mowing free, relate to so much of that 'school stuff'? This is not to say that classroom experiences are any less 'real' than experiences outside school contexts. Nor is it to deny that many teachers *do* work hard at trying to prepare students for the world beyond schooling.

If we are stuck in some kind of 'skills and processes' view of literacy we may not be able to understand the depth of such matters and to respond to them in practice. Of course, the sociocultural view does not deny the importance of encoding and decoding skills! Not at all. It just recognises that there is much more to literacy. It insists on teaching and developing these skills and processes within contexts that are meaningful to learners, in that second sense of 'meaningful': within practices that 'connect with' and 'hook into' the experiences and worlds of learners.

Getting more *out of* Jacques in class would require getting more of *Jacques* into the learning context: more of what he *is* and what he *knows*.

The limits to 'making it explicit'

The case of Jacques should stimulate us to think about just what can and cannot be achieved in literacy education by the notion of 'making it explicit'. This is a very important pedagogical principle. It means that we should 'spell out' and 'bring to the surface' as concretely and tangibly as we can those things that underlie the learning task and the thing to be learned. In the case of mastering different 'genres', for instance, it is not a matter simply of 'throwing learners into the genre' and hoping that it will 'stick'. We need to identify and clarify the language and contextual features of the genre and try to relate it to purposes and contexts as tangibly as possible: so that learners will not only (ideally) 'know how to do it', but also 'know what it is that they know how to do'. But even if we do this very well, it might not be enough to get the results we seek.

In Jacques' case, the teacher was practically bending over backwards to make 'scaffolding' strategies and concepts like 'compare and contrast' explicit. But it simply was not registering with Jacques. This, I believe, is because the gap between the nature of the school literacy tasks and Jacques' prior experience and 'literacy blueprints' was too wide. For something to become or be made explicit—such as the purpose of being able to use compare and contrast strategies in essay writing—there has to be a lot of relevant cultural and social learning already in place for the 'explicitness' to hook onto. There are two ways in which this might be achieved. One is where learners bring with them to school the kinds of prior experiences that mesh well with school tasks. The other, which is what applies to cases like Jacques, is by trying to shift the 'school literacy activity' onto more familiar terrain for the learner. Jacques, for instance, knew perfectly well how to compare and contrast within particular contexts of social practice. He didn't use a tangible 'template' like the teacher's proforma, but he certainly used 'templates' constructed out of his purposes, priorities and values when it came to making decisions about things that were important. For Jacques' teacher, trying to make the classroom tasks and learnings explicit would have to begin with building connections from 'Jacques space' to 'class space'.

In cases we can think of from our own experience, what might this involve, how well do we do it, and how well can we do it?

The literate 'subject'

Much of our current educational theory and practice is based on the assumption that it is *individuals* who learn and come to know things. This assumption is built deeply into our assessment and into our reporting of 'competencies', 'achievement' and the like. It is also built deeply into our assumptions about teaching and learning—such as in catering for individual differences. Indeed, we have drawn attention to the need to factor individual (and group) differences into literacy work.

At the same time, we should maintain a healthy scepticism about some of the lengths to which we push this individualistic emphasis in education. In the work world, increasing emphasis is being given to work *teams*. Many jobs are done by teams as a whole, and efficiency, productivity—and rewards—are measured and distributed on a team basis. We find more and more theorists talking about 'distributed expertise'. Indeed, we can readily recognise that nothing can be achieved in literacy by individuals on their own. Every literate production is a joint production. Yet, when it comes to assessing learning, we fall back on the individual.

In the case of Jacques, we have stunning examples of collaborative and cooperative 'literacy productions' that are successful, and that add depth and meaning to human relationships. The mowing service flier was a collaborative production which, in its making, embodied a good deal of 'truth' about the home culture. It was an authentic business artefact produced by the very people who identify with the family business (Dad's computer, Mum's and his brother's assistance, shared knowledge and expertise). This was a 'truly real' literacy event and production. How many of our school productions can we say this for? And to what extent is our inability to claim 'realness' and 'authenticity' for so much school literacy a consequence of our involvement in distorting a collaborative social practice (language and literacy) by twisting it into teaching and learning frames that are driven by the assumption that 'assessment shall be of the individual', and that literacy shall be a 'private, personal, individual possession'?

Most importantly of all, what is to be done about this within our school language and literacy planning and programming? What is the 'right' balance between individual and group or community practice when it comes to assessing literacy achievement? What kind of assessment activities would be required to do justice to the status of literacy as an 'embedded social and cultural (as opposed simply to *textual*) practice'?

Has Jacques 'got it right'?

James Gee makes some important and interesting points about learning in general and literacy learning in particular. First, he says that meaningful learning—that is, sensible and purposeful learning—is always about 'a process of entry into and participation in a Discourse' (Gee, Hull and Lankshear 1996: 15). By 'Discourse' here we can simply see Jacques' social involvement in Theocratic School and in 'witnessing' as components of his church/religion Discourse. In this sense, learning is about becoming capable of taking on social roles and identities that others can recognise, and of knowing how to 'do these correctly'. In Jacques' case, 'witnessing' doesn't just involve the language bits of talking about literature and social issues, but also about how he dresses and carries himself (including the briefcase). What Jacques prepares for and does in Theocratic School and on his witnessing circuits is part of his learning to be a Jehovah's Witness. And anyone who is 'on the inside' of this Discourse would be able to identify Jacques readily as a Jehovah's Witness from what he does and the way he does certain things. Which is simply to say that Jacques has learned a great deal successfully about this Discourse.

Second, Gee says that when we look at effective learning from a sociocultural viewpoint, with the emphasis on becoming competent at Discourses, we have to acknowledge that the focus of learning is on 'human lives seen as *trajectories* through multiple social practices in various social institutions'. We learn today for things that we will do and be tomorrow (in the future). This means that what a learner does *now* as a learner 'must be connected in meaningful and motivating ways with 'mature' versions of related social practices'. By 'mature' versions of social practice, Gee means 'the real thing', the 'real McCoy'. While the things we do in school literacy and learning today may relate well to things we learn and do later *within school*, it is a further question how far it relates to anything else (Gee, Hull and Lankshear 1996: 4).

When Jacques is in Theocratic School, he isn't in 'school'. He is in 'the real thing'. What he is learning to do are the things that 'real' Jehovah's Witnesses do, and the way that they do them—as adult Jehovah's Witnesses. What he is learning to do in producing his flier is similarly a very close approximation to what 'real' small businesses do to drum up business.

But how much of our schooling is like this? How 'real' was the writers' centre? How 'real' are so many of the literacy activities we engage learners in within classrooms? What relationship, if any, do they have to the 'mature' versions of social practices we engage in later in life, later in our trajectories? What are we leaving out in our current offerings? What are we distorting? How wide is the gap between what we teach and learn in 'the literacy classroom' and the 'mature' practices of producing, say, newspaper reports or research projects? How can we reduce the gap?

And was Jacques expressing something very profound when he lampooned the story publishing process?

Conclusion

I'm not advancing any of the above as 'fixed truths' or as 'the right way to look at and do things', and I've certainly raised more questions in this chapter than answered them. Rather, my point has been to try and create a space from which we can look at our ideas and practices from a different point of view, and to see some of the ways in which we, as educators, might create such spaces for ourselves from which to *reflect critically* on literacy and literacy education. My hope is that this chapter provides some incentive and some guidelines for engaging in critical reflection on literacy and classroom literacy practices. By reflecting on their own classroom literacy practices and the questions generated by the case of Jacques, teachers can begin to develop their own set of 'guidelines' that will inform the criteria they use to 'judge' and construct equitably or 'morally just' literacy practices in their classrooms. For now and the foreseeable future, literacy and literacy education will be so important that they justify all the critical reflective energies we can muster.

References

Gee, J P (1996) *Social Linguistics and Literacies: Ideology in Discourses*. 2nd edn. London: Taylor and Francis.
Gee, J P, Hull, G and Lankshear, C (1996) *The New Work Order: Behind the Language of the New Capitalism*. Sydney and Boulder, Colarado: Allen and Unwin and Westview Press.
Heath, S B (1982) 'What no bedtime story means: Narrative skills at home and school', *Language and Society*. Vol. 11, pp 49–76.
Heath, S B (1983) *Ways With Words: Language, Life and Work in Community and Classrooms*. Cambridge: Cambridge University Press.
Hill, S, Comber, B, Louden, W, Rivalland, J and Reid, J (1998) *100 Children go to School: Connections and Disconnections in Literacy Development in the Year Prior to School and the First Year of School*. Canberra: DEETYA.
Knobel, M (1997). *Language and Social Practices in Four Adolescents' Everyday Lives*. PhD thesis. Brisbane: QUT, Faculty of Education.
Knobel, M (1998) *Everyday Literacies*. New York: Peter Lang Publishing.
Michaels, S (1981) '"Sharing time": Children's narrative styles and differential access to literacy', *Language in Society*. Vol 10, pp 423–442.

Michaels, S (1985). 'Hearing the connections in children's oral and written discourse', *Journal of Education*. Vol 167, pp 36–56.
Yeager, B, Floriani, A and Green, J (1998) 'Learning to see learning in the classroom: Developing an ethnographic perspective', in A Egan-Robertson and D Bloome (eds) *Students as Researchers of Culture and Language in their Own Communities*. Cresskill, New Jersey: Hampton Press.

Glossary

MICHELE KNOBEL AND EILEEN HONAN

Binaries
Opposites; eg male/female, strong/weak, hard/soft. Feminist poststructuralists attempt to 'disrupt and deconstruct the binarisms through which we structure our knowledge of ourselves and the social world. Binary thought is absolutely fundamental to the maintenance of the male/female dualism' (Davies 1994: 8). Part of this binary thought is the actual structure of the binary pairs; for example in those listed above, the ascendant category, or most powerful position, is listed first.

Code/s
In the sense used in this book, 'codes' refer to the language system, which includes the grammatical system but not necessarily the meaning system of language. Refer to Allan Luke and Peter Freebody's description of four elements of reading below (ie found under 'text user').

Constructs
Social construction: 'literacy is not just the simple ability to read and write: but by possessing and performing these skills we exercise socially approved and approvable talents; in other words, literacy is a socially constructed phenomenon' (Cook-Gumperz 1986: 1). This construction occurs through social interaction, negotiating meanings in different contexts. Contexts, in the sense used in this book, are more than the physical sites of events. They are spaces of negotiation, interaction, and action that occur within, and in relation to, sites. As such, contexts are coordinated always by social, historical and political forces and events. An example of a social construction is the notion of a reading 'age' that is based on the assumption that even a few months makes all the difference to a child's reading ability.

Texts as constructs: Texts—or the meanings and readings of texts—are also socially constructed. The construction of a meaning of a particular text is affected by the social interactions and contexts in which the reading (and writing) occurs.

Critical literacy
Although this book is devoted to explaining and exemplifying the complex concepts and practices constituting 'critical literacy', it sometimes helps to have a shorthand definition. For our purposes, then, we define critical literacy as the analysis and critique of the relationships among language, power, social groups and social practices.

Critical pedagogy
'Critical pedagogy is designed to give students the tools to examine how society has functioned to shape and constrain their aspirations and goals, and prevent them from even dreaming about a life outside the one they presently know (Giroux 1981)' (Darder 1991: xvii). Critical pedagogy describes the teaching strategies and practices used to promote and enact critical literacy in the classroom.

Critical reading
Reading texts critically is about bringing their ideologies into the open, addressing our own role in relation to the production or promotion of these texts, and working to 'remove our moral complicity' (Gee 1996: 21) when our analysis and critique shows that the texts we are reading work to advantage us, and to disadvantage others. For example, reading critically could include analysing the links between a text where the female character is never given a name and wider social contexts that operate to make women 'invisible' (eg factory outsourcing for designer clothes labels).

Critical thinking
Critical thinking in the literacy arena is generally associated with psychological 'takes' on 'doing things with texts'. Synonymous terms include 'metacognition', and it can include higher order thinking processes, top level structures, and other schemas designed to assist effective

thinking. More specifically, Richard Paul (1995), from the *Center for Critical Thinking* (USA), defines critical thinking as 'the ability to think about one's thinking in such a way as (1) to recognize its strengths and weaknesses and, as a result, (2) to recast the thinking in improved form' (source: http://www.sonoma.edu/cthink/definect.html cited July 7, 1998). This includes remembering facts, effectively using habits of thinking that require little effort, inquiry (to reach sound conclusions), generating new ideas and being creative (OISE 1997). In addition, critical thinking is part and parcel of the act of 'processing information', which includes 'knowledge application, analysis, synthesis, reasoning, problem solving, decision making, and evaluation' (Crowley 1996).

Cultural capital

The term 'cultural capital' is used to signal group and individual differences in power and status that are the 'result' of different representations of 'culture' (Bourdieu 1986). Cultural capital refers to what Bourdieu calls 'embodied competence', which he uses as a coverall term for the cultural knowledge and practices a person enacts in her everyday life. James Paul Gee (1996: 8) talks about cultural capital in terms of primary Discourse; that is, our 'initial taken-for-granted understandings of *who* we are and *who* people 'like us' are, as well as what sorts of things ("people like us") do, value, and believe' [original emphases]. Thus in schooling, certain sets of cultural knowledge and practices are accorded higher status (ie value) than others, which necessarily disadvantages certain groups over others. Generally, the culture of the dominant social group is most valued in education (see Heath 1983). For example, the ability to sit still and attend while a teacher is reading a book to the class, is generally valued by teachers over actions that disrupt the reading (eg commenting without being asked to do so, linking this text to other texts without being asked to do so, pointing to pictures and so on without being asked to do so). Generally, students that 'know' this about the culture of the classroom will be seen to be 'successful' or 'good' students; and often, this knowledge comes from their own membership in a particular culture that values similar things that are valued in the classroom culture.

Essentialism

'Essentialism is classically defined as a belief in true essence—that which is most irreducible, unchanging, and therefore constitutive of a given person or thing' (Fuss 1990: 2). For example, in feminist theory essentialism refers to beliefs in a pure essence of femininity; that there is a core of 'femaleness' that is unaltered by social constructs.

Genres

Genres are characterised in the literature as staged, goal-oriented, social processes: 'They are referred to as *social processes* because members of a culture interact with each other to achieve them; as *goal-oriented* because they have evolved to get things done; and as *staged* because it usually takes more than one step for participants to achieve their goals' (Martin, Christie, and Rothery 1987: 59; original emphases). In literacy education, however, 'genre' is usually used to refer to types of texts and their social purpose(s).

Ideology

'Ideology' is itself a contested term. For present purposes, we describe ideology as a social theory or worldview that involves generalisations (beliefs, claims) about the ways in which the world 'works' (see Gee 1996: 21). Ideologies are tied closely to distributions of power and access to goods and services in any society. Think, for example, of the far reaching effects of the long-prevailing and widely held ideology that failure at school is the sole fault of the individual.

Normative (role)

Norm; normativity. This concept is used to signal the work certain social conventions, assumptions, and practices *do* in regulating and differentiating between 'desirable' and 'undesirable' activity, talk etc. Norms are social constructions (see above) and change over time and across social groups and cultures. In critical literacy literature, 'normative' is used generally as a negative term in describing the ways in which social, language, and institutional practices (and values, beliefs, actions etc) are coordinated by dominant ideologies. Think of events in your own life where you have been disciplined—in subtle or overt ways—for thinking and acting differently, and the effects this had on you.

Positioning and reading positions
'Texts construct a particular view of the world by providing a certain reading position from where the text seems unproblematic and natural' (Kress 1985: 36). The concept of 'reader position' is linked to the notion of the 'ideal reader' (ie generally approached as the kind of reader the author most likely had in mind when constructing a text). For example, the 'ideal reader' of a *Goosebumps* book is someone who reads it without questioning or feeling uncomfortable about the author's view of the world.

Social practice(s)
Social practices are 'regular patterning of actions' (Lemke 1995: 102). This patterning is socially constituted over time by repeated and recognised ways of doing things. The meaning of a social practice is conferred by the shared purposes, values, beliefs and so forth of those people participating—and not participating—in it (Knobel 1998).

Systemic functional linguistics
This method of linguistic analysis was developed by Michael Halliday (1985) as a *systematic* framework for describing language and the ways in which it *functions* in cultural and situational contexts. It provides a metalanguage—a language for talking about language—that aims to be as descriptive as possible (eg *material processes* refer to words that indicate some sort of physical or observable action—run, skip, chew etc).

Texts
Although some theorists conceptualise 'text' very broadly; in this book we subscribe to Gunther Kress' conception of texts as 'relevant units of language' (1985: 31).

Text user, participant, code breaker [and analyst]
Luke and Freebody (1997) describe the four elements of reading as a social practice. In this model reading involves coding practices, text-meaning practices, pragmatic practices and critical practices. Readers are active agents who use cultural resources to break codes, participate in and use text, and critically analyse texts (see also Freebody 1992).

Worldview
The pattern of beliefs, assumptions, theories and so on that construct a particular version—or view—of the world for individuals and groups of people. For example, political parties construct and promote a particular view or version of the world on which to base and justify their claims and policies.

References

Bourdieu, P (1986) *Distinction: A Social Critique of the Judgement of Taste*. Trans R Nice. London: Routledge.

Cook-Gumperz, J (1986) (ed) *The Social Construction of Literacy*. Cambridge: Cambridge University Press.

Crowley, J (1996) Critical Thinking in the Laboratory: Key Word List. Cited 8 July, 1998. http://158.93.30.93/MedTech/LL/CT/KEYWORDS.HTM

Darder, A (1991) *Culture and Power in the Classroom: A Critical Foundation for Bicultural Education*. New York: Bergin and Garvey.

Davies, B (1994) *Poststructuralist Theory and Classroom Practice*. Geelong: Deakin University Press.

Freebody, P (1992) 'A socio-cultural approach: Resourcing four roles as a literacy learner', in A Watson and A Badenhop (eds) *Prevention of Reading Failure*. Sydney: Ashton Scholastic, pp 48–60.

Fuss, D (1989) *Essentially Speaking*. New York: Routledge.

Gee, J (1996) *Social Linguistics and Literacies: Ideology in Discourses*, 2nd edn. London: Falmer Press.

Heath, S (1983) *Ways With Words: Language, Life and Work in Community and Classrooms*. Cambridge: Cambridge University Press.

Knobel, M (1998) *Everyday Literacies: Students, Discourses, and Social Practices*. New York: Peter Lang.

Kress, G (1985) *Linguistic Processes in Sociocultural Practice*. Geelong: Deakin University Press.

Lemke, J (1995) *Textual Politics*. London: Taylor and Francis.

Luke, A and Freebody P (1997) 'Shaping the social practices of reading', in S Muspratt, A Luke, and P Freebody (eds) *Constructing Critical Literacies: Teaching and Learning Textual Practice*. Cresskill, New Jersey: Hampton Press.

Halliday, M (1985) *An Introduction to Functional Grammar*. London: Edward Arnold.

Martin, J, Christie, F and Rothery, J (1987) 'Social processes in education: A reply to Sawyer and Watson (and others)', in I Reid (ed) *The Place of Genre in Learning: Current Debates*. Geelong: Centre for Studies in Literacy Education, Deakin University.

OISE (Ontario Institute for Studies in Education) (1997) Critical Thinking. Cited July 8, 1998. http://www3.sympatico.ca/lgrightmire/CRITICAL.HTM

Paul, R (1995) Three Definitions of Critical Thinking. Cited 7 July, 1998. http://www.sonoma.edu/cthink/definect.html